James C. Miller

Introduction
to Compiler Construction
with UNIX

Introduction
to Compiler Construction
with UNIX*

Axel T. Schreiner
Sektion Informatik
University of Ulm, West Germany

H. George Friedman, Jr.
Department of Computer Science
University of Illinois at Urbana-Champaign

Prentice-Hall, Inc.
Englewood Cliffs, NJ 07632

UNIX is a trademark of Bell Laboratories.

Library of Congress Catalog Card Number: 84-63039

Editorial/production supervision:
  Sophia Papanikolaou/Barbara Palumbo
Cover design: Lundgren Graphics
Manufacturing buyer: Gordon Osbourne

UNIX is a trademark of Bell Laboratories.

Prentice-Hall Software Series, Brian W. Kernighan, advisor.

Printed in the United States of America

10 9 8 7 6 5 4 3 2 1

ISBN 0-13-474396-2   01

PRENTICE-HALL INTERNATIONAL, INC., *London*
PRENTICE-HALL OF AUSTRALIA PTY. LIMITED, *Sydney*
EDITORA PRENTICE-HALL DO BRASIL, LTDA., *Rio de Janeiro*
PRENTICE-HALL CANADA INC., *Toronto*
PRENTICE-HALL HISPANOAMERICANA, S.A., *Mexico*
PRENTICE-HALL OF INDIA PRIVATE LIMITED, *New Delhi*
PRENTICE-HALL OF JAPAN, INC., *Tokyo*
PRENTICE-HALL OF SOUTHEAST ASIA PTE. LTD., *Singapore*
WHITEHALL BOOKS LIMITED, *Wellington, New Zealand*

To Carol and Claudia,
who put up with us.

Contents

Introduction

Better user interfaces, especially to the many micro computers which are becoming so popular, often require recognition and processing of rather elaborate command languages. Language recognition thus has many applications. However, it can be downright unpleasant if done *ad-hack*. Building a compiler illustrates one application of language recognition. It also illustrates how to design and implement a large program with tools and successive extensions of a basic design. Understanding a simple compiler is interesting in its own right: it helps one to master and better utilize programming systems in general.

This book is a case study: how to create a compiler using generators such as *yacc* (LALR(1) parser generator) and *lex* (regular expression based lexical analyzer generator), two very powerful yet reasonably easy to use tools available under the UNIX† system.

A very simple subset of C, called *sampleC*, is defined and used as an example for compiler development. The resulting implementation of *sampleC* is not intended as an end in itself, and is therefore allowed to produce less than optimal object code. Suggestions for improvements to the code and extensions to the language are given as problems for the reader in several chapters.

The text largely avoids theoretical details, such as detailed discussion of grammars, or explanations of the internal workings of the generators, but it does suggest readings. It explains at least the simpler aspects of using the generators.

As a result, on one level we present a tutorial on how to use the generators to get a simple, easily modifiable implementation done quickly and reliably. On another level, the reader learns practical details about the components of a compiler and the customary interfaces between them.

As such, the text is intended both as a short exposition preceding detailed algorithm studies in compiler construction, and as a description of how to productively employ the generators described. It is not intended to be a comprehensive treatment of the subject of compiler design. Neither does it discuss all aspects of using the generators; once the text has been read, the original descriptions of the generators [Joh78] and [Les78b] are accessible, and they are intended to be used as references to accompany the text. Since a compiler is a large program, the text demonstrates how such a program can be structured and designed with attention to debugging, extension, and maintenance issues.

The reader is expected to have a working knowledge of an editor, of the host machine's file system manipulations, and — of course — of C, in which all the examples are written. Knowledge of other languages, such as Pascal, Fortran, or Basic, would also be useful to the reader. An understanding of block structured languages such as C and their scope rules, and of data structures such as stacks, is important beginning with chapter 5. Some experience with a pattern matching editor is assumed in chapter 2.

---

† UNIX is a trademark of Bell Laboratories.

A few words about terminology. We make a careful distinction between the *declaration* of a variable, function, label, or other program element, and the *definition* of that element. A declaration is merely a statement that a program element exists and has certain characteristics, such as the type of a variable, the types of the parameters and return value of a function, etc. A definition gives substance to a declared program element, by providing a value for a variable, a body of code for a function, a location for a label, etc.

In discussing grammars, we have departed slightly from traditional terminology. We prefer to avoid the word *production* and the terms *right hand side* and *left hand side*. Instead, we refer to a *rule*, by which we mean *all* of the productions (and the alternative right hand sides) of a given non-terminal symbol, and to a *formulation*, by which we mean *one* of the alternatives on the right hand side of a rule.

Machine readable source files for the examples in this book can be obtained from the second author, e.g., over ARPANET, BITNET, CSNET, or USENET.

We would like to thank the reviewer for his constructive suggestions. We also gratefully acknowledge the use of the computer facilities of the Computer Science Department of the University of Illinois at Urbana-Champaign, which are supported in part by NSF grant MCS 81-05896, and of the Sektion Informatik of the University of Ulm, with which this book was developed, composed, and typeset.

ATS
HGF
Urbana, Illinois

Chapter 1
Language Definition

A compiler accepts a *source program* — a program written in some *source language* — and constructs an equivalent *object program* written in an *object language*, such as assembler language or binary machine language. In other words, a compiler must recognize an input source program and check it for consistency of grammar and meaning, then compose an equivalent object program.

Before we can build a compiler, we need to discuss the mechanics of language definition. The present chapter will describe methods of specifying the grammar of a source language, and of checking the correctness of that grammar. The next chapter will show how the individual "words" of the source language can be recognized. In chapter 3, we will combine these two aspects of a compiler so that it can recognize a correct source program, and in chapter 4, we will extend it so that it can do something "reasonable" even with an incorrect source program. Subsequent chapters will show how to save information needed during compilation and how to use this information to finally generate an object program.

1.1 Purpose

Two aspects constitute a language definition: *syntax* and *semantics*. The syntax deals with the mechanical aspects, namely whether or not a sequence of words (or letters) is a *sentence* in the language. What the sentence means — and sometimes whether it is legitimate on that account — is determined by the semantics of the language.

Formal notations exist for both parts of the language definition. The syntax is usually explained through a sequence of models describing the parts of a sentence. *Syntax graphs*, pioneered by Wirth in the definition of Pascal, are drawn like flowcharts:

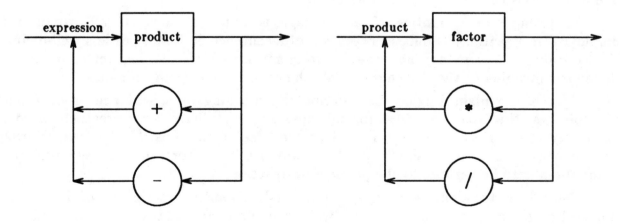

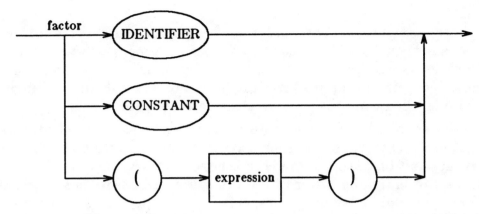

Backus Naur Form (BNF) is a language in which the syntax of a language (even of BNF itself) can be specified:

```
expression
        : expression '+' product
        | expression '-' product
        | product

product
        : product '*' factor
        | product '/' factor
        | factor

factor
        : IDENTIFIER
        | CONSTANT
        | '(' expression ')'
```

We will discuss BNF in more detail later.

Describing the semantics of a language is much harder. If a formalism is employed, it essentially simulates execution of a sentence on a more or less well-defined theoretical machine model, and the resulting machine states — legitimate or not — define the meaning of the sentence, or rule the sentence out as meaningless.

We can use plain English to describe the meaning of a sentence or of a part thereof. In the absence of a formal notation, simplicity and precision become extremely important — Wirth's Pascal or Modula-2 definitions, [Jen75] and [Wir82], are very good examples, and just about any PL/I or Fortran language reference manual tends to be verbose to the point of destruction.

There is a tradeoff between syntactic and semantic description of limitations imposed on a sentence. Consider, e.g., Basic, where an `identifier` can be defined as

```
id
        : LETTER DIGIT
        | LETTER

identifier
        : id '$'
        | id
```

If the operator + is used for addition between numerical values *and* for concatenation between strings, the semantic description must state that + may not be used to "add" a string to a numerical value or vice versa.

Alternatively, we can define

```
real_id
        : LETTER DIGIT
        | LETTER

string_id
        : real_id '$'
```

In this fashion we can distinguish string and numerical computations in a purely syntactic fashion throughout the language definition.

A Basic `identifier` is certainly a borderline case between what can (and should) be specified syntactically, and what can (and should) be specified semantically. In general in defining a language, we should not do in English what can be done (sensibly) in a more formal way.

1.2 Mechanical aspects

BNF is a formalism to describe the syntax of a language. It was pioneered by Peter Naur in the Algol 60 Report [Nau63] and has since been used to describe numerous languages. It has also been extended and overloaded, perhaps to a point where the resulting description is no longer easily grasped [Wij75].

A *grammar*, the BNF description of a language, consists of a sequence of *rules*. A rule consists of a *left-hand side* and a *right-hand side*, separated by a colon. The left-hand side consists of a single, unique *non-terminal symbol*[1]. The right-hand side consists of a sequence of one or more *formulations*, separated from one another by a bar. Each formulation consists of a sequence of zero or more non-terminal and *terminal* symbols. Only one formulation in a rule may be empty; since this can be the only formulation in the rule, the entire right-hand side may be empty. An example of a grammar was shown in section 1.1:

```
expression
        : expression '+' product
        | expression '-' product
        | product

product
        : product '*' factor
        | product '/' factor
        | factor

factor
        : IDENTIFIER
        | CONSTANT
        | '(' expression ')'
```

---

[1] We only discuss context-free language definitions in a very informal manner. For a comprehensive treatment consult, e.g., [Aho77].

A grammar defines a language by explaining which sentences may be formed. The non-terminal symbol on the left-hand side of the first rule is termed the *start symbol*. Here the start symbol is expression. The first rule lists all possible formulations for the start symbol. Each formulation may introduce new non-terminal symbols, such as product in this example.

For each non-terminal, a rule must exist, and any one of the formulations from this rule can be substituted for the non-terminal. Substitution continues until a sequence of terminal symbols, a *sentence*, is *produced* from the start symbol of the grammar. The terminal symbols are not further explained in the grammar; they are the alphabet in which are written the sentences of the language which the grammar describes.

Once the rules of the grammar involve non-terminal symbols in a recursive fashion, infinitely many — and infinitely long — sentences are possible. In our example we have, e.g., the following sentence:

IDENTIFIER

by choosing the formulations product for expression, factor for product, and IDENTIFIER for factor. Another example is

IDENTIFIER * (CONSTANT + IDENTIFIER)

Here, we must use number of intermediate formulations before we can conclude that this is in fact a sentence described by the grammar. It is customary to arrange these formulations as a *parse tree*. The root of this ordered tree is labeled with the start symbol of the grammar. The leaves are, in order, labeled with the terminal symbols of a sentence. Each non-terminal node is labeled with a non-terminal symbol, and the branches from a node lead to nodes which, in order, are labeled with the symbols from a formulation of this non-terminal.

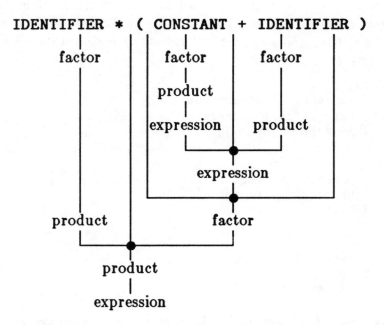

BNF is itself a language and can be described in BNF:

```
grammar
        : grammar rule
        | rule

rule

        : rule '|' formulation
        | NONTERMINAL ':' formulation
        | NONTERMINAL ':'

formulation
        : formulation symbol
        | symbol

symbol

        : NONTERMINAL
        | TERMINAL
```

This description is slightly more restrictive than the informal definition given above: here an empty formulation must be the first one in a rule. (Why?!)

As the examples show, recursion plays a major role in BNF. Rules are usually written in a *left-recursive* fashion — the non-terminal to be formulated appears again at the beginning of one of its own formulations, thus giving rise to an infinitely long sequence of like phrases. This technique tends to obscure simple situations, and especially language reference manuals therefore extend BNF with iterative constructs such as brackets [and] to enclose optional items and braces { and } to enclose items which may appear zero or more times. Sometimes parentheses are also employed, to introduce precedence and factor the selection operation (bar) and normal concatenation of symbols in a sequence. Extended BNF (or one variant thereof) can be included in our description of BNF. We merely need to replace the rule for symbol by the following:

```
symbol
        : NONTERMINAL
        | TERMINAL
        | '{' formulation '}'
        | '[' formulation ']'
```

Our grammar for arithmetic expressions can then be modified:

```
expression
        : product { '+' product }
        | product { '-' product }

product
        : factor { '*' factor }
        | factor { '/' factor }
```

factor remains as above.

Extended BNF can describe itself:

```
grammar
        : rule { rule }

rule
        : NONTERMINAL ':' [ formulation ] { '|' formulation }

formulation
        : symbol { symbol }

symbol
        : NONTERMINAL
        | TERMINAL
        | '{' formulation '}'
        | '[' formulation ']'
```

Our discussion has been quite informal. Still, a word on representation is perhaps in order: *non-terminal symbols* are specified like identifiers in a programming language — they consist of letters and possibly digits and underscores; they start with a letter. *terminal symbols* tend to be spelled in upper case; if they are single special characters, we enclose them in single quotes. White space (spaces and tabs) is usually insignificant, and merely serves to delimit other symbols.

1.3 Convenient grammars

If we define a language to be a set of sentences, i.e., of sequences of terminal symbols, there are usually many ways to define a grammar describing the language. While a language need not be finite, a grammar is by definition required to be finite. This restriction alone, however, is not sufficient. Consider the following two grammars describing very simple arithmetic expressions:

```
expression
        : expression '-' IDENTIFIER
        | IDENTIFIER
```

and

```
expression
        : IDENTIFIER '-' expression
        | IDENTIFIER
```

For both grammars, the language consists of all alternating sequences of IDENTIFIER and −. There is an important difference, which we can see if we compare the parse trees for an expression:

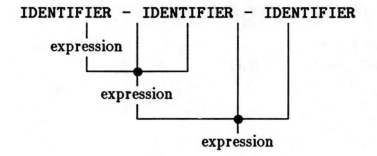

The left-recursive grammar collects terminal symbols beginning on the left; the right-recursive grammar builds (in this case) a mirror image of the first parse tree:

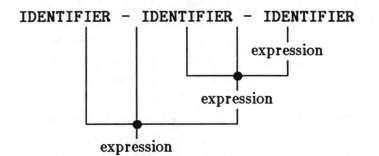

In the context of arithmetic expressions, the parse tree is *interpreted* to also describe precedence and associativity of operators, i.e., to define the order in which the terms of an arithmetic expression need to be combined for evaluation. This example introduces only one operator and there is therefore no precedence problem. Depending on the grammar, however, we would introduce different ways to implicitly parenthesize: the left-recursive grammar implies that the operator − is left-associative, i.e., is implicitly parenthesized from the left, and the right-recursive grammar implies the insertion of parentheses from the right. Most operators are left-associative and must therefore be introduced using left recursion.

Unfortunately, this is not the only problem. Consider the following proposal for a grammar, still for the same language of arithmetic expressions:

```
expression
        : expression '-' expression
        | IDENTIFIER
```

With this rule, we can build *either* parse tree shown above. The grammar is therefore called *ambiguous*: there exists a sentence in the language for which two different parse trees may be built. Ambiguity is often a property of the grammar, not usually of the language. As the previous examples indicate, there exist non-ambiguous grammars for the same language. We can make the proposal unambiguous by insisting that the parse tree must be built up starting on the left — this condition is known as a *disambiguating rule*.

As a first task, a compiler must recognize the language it is to translate, i.e., for every sequence of terminal symbols, it must be able to determine efficiently whether or not it is a sentence of the language. The problem can be dealt with by attempting to build a parse tree. If we have an unambiguous grammar for the language, we can begin with its start symbol, try each formulation in turn, substitute for each non-terminal, and attempt to arrive at a parse tree for a proposed sentence. In an organized fashion, this amounts to backtracking and is thus inherently inefficient. Additionally, if the compiler produces output while it constructs the parse tree, backtracking cannot even be readily accomplished, since it would involve undoing some of the output!

A convenient grammar for language recognition must not only be unambiguous, it must be deterministic: the as yet unused rest of the input, i.e., the tail of the sequence of terminal symbols proposed as a sentence, together with the partially constructed parse tree, must enable us to uniquely decide which rule and formulation to use in order to complete the parse tree if it exists, or to discover that no tree can be constructed to accommodate the next input symbol.

Different notions of convenience exist, depending largely on the ingenuity of the compiler writer and the power of his tools. A simple sufficient condition is, for example, that each formulation start in a unique terminal symbol. In this case the next, single input symbol determines what needs to be done.

The grammars for modern programming languages tend to follow a less restrictive pattern: they usually possess the LL(1) or LR(1) property, or variants thereof. In the first case, a parse tree can be built top-down without backtracking; in the second case, the parse tree can be built bottom-up without backtracking using certain tables, for which construction programs exist. In each case we only need to know the *next* input symbol at all times, i.e., we require *one symbol look-ahead*.

The LL(1) property is simply this: whenever there is a question as to which rule or which formulation to use, the next input symbol must enable us to uniquely decide what to do. The question arises when we need to choose one of several formulations in a rule. If none of the formulations is empty, each starts either in a terminal or in a non-terminal symbol. The next input symbol can be one of these terminal symbols; alternatively, considering recursively all the formulations for all the (first) non-terminal symbols, we arrive at more terminal symbols at the beginning of formulations. The next input symbol *must* be *exactly one* of these terminal symbols, which therefore must all be different. If there is an empty formulation, we need to additionally consider the initial terminal symbols of all the formulations for non-terminal symbols which can *follow* in the present situation.

Deciding the LL(1) property is not really difficult, since it can be phrased in terms of relations such as *a terminal symbol starts a formulation for a non-terminal symbol* and *two symbols follow each other in a formulation*. Such relations can be expressed as Boolean matrices [Gri71], and more complicated relations can be composed and computed. Using the LL(1) property is even easier: once a grammar is LL(1), a recursive recognizer for its language can be built in a very straightforward manner; see [Wir77].

Even if a grammar is definitely not LL(1), certain semantic tricks can be used to make language recognition deterministic. Consider a simplified excerpt for Pascal:

```
statement
        : IDENTIFIER ':=' expression
        | IDENTIFIER
```

The first formulation describes an assignment, the second one a procedure call. Both versions of IDENTIFIER being equal, a name as next input symbol would not decide which formulation is to be used. The problem is usually circumvented by recognizing that only a *procedure* IDENTIFIER can start a procedure call; such an IDENTIFIER can, however, not start an assignment. Since in Pascal names need to be declared before they can be used, we can solve our syntactic problem with a semantic trick.

1.4 Checking a grammar

A compiler must decide whether or not a sequence of terminal symbols is a sentence of a language. A grammar describes a language. A natural question is whether we can use a grammar more or less directly in the recognition process.

First of all, however, the grammar should be checked: there must be rules for all non-terminals, all non-terminals must be reachable from the start symbol, and the grammar should satisfy a property such as LL(1) so that it is suitable for recognition and not ambiguous.

Johnson's *yacc*, a powerful utility in the UNIX system [Joh78], can be used to check a grammar in this fashion. *yacc* accepts a grammar specified in BNF and (for the present discussion) will indicate any problems which make the grammar unsuitable for language recognition. As an example, we prepare the following input file *grammar*:

```
/*
 *      first example of a yacc grammar
 */

%token  IDENTIFIER

%%

expression
        : expression '-' IDENTIFIER
        | IDENTIFIER
```

and test it with the command

```
yacc grammar
```

Nothing happens, and this is as it should be — the grammar is acceptable according to *yacc*. Actually, there will be a new file *y.tab.c*, which will be discussed in chapter 3.

As the example shows, input to *yacc* uses the representation for BNF discussed earlier. Since terminal symbols and non-terminal symbols look alike, *yacc* requires that the terminal symbols be defined using %token specifications prior to the actual grammar. A line containing %% must separate the two parts of the input file[2]. White space and C-style comments are ignored.

On a more technical level, let us look at how *yacc* checks a grammar. (The computational aspects of this are discussed by Horning in chapter 2.C. in [Bau76] or in [Aho74].) *yacc* has what amounts to an option for debugging a grammar; if we issue the command

```
yacc -v grammar
```

we obtain the following file *y.output*:

```
state 0
        $accept : _expression $end
```

---

[2] We will introduce the relevant aspects of the input language for *yacc* as we go along. As a reference, the reader is referred to [Joh78].

```
              IDENTIFIER  shift 2
                 error

              expression  goto 1

      state 1
              $accept : expression_$end
              expression : expression_- IDENTIFIER

              $end  accept
              -  shift 3
              .  error


      state 2
              expression : IDENTIFIER_     (2)

              .  reduce 2


      state 3
              expression : expression -_IDENTIFIER

              IDENTIFIER  shift 4
              .  error


      state 4
              expression : expression - IDENTIFIER_     (1)

              .  reduce 1


    4/127 terminals, 1/175 nonterminals
    3/350 grammar rules, 5/550 states
    0 shift/reduce, 0 reduce/reduce conflicts reported
    3/225 working sets used
    memory: states,etc. 26/4500, parser 0/3500
    3/400 distinct lookahead sets
    0 extra closures
    3 shift entries, 1 exceptions
    1 goto entries
    0 entries saved by goto default
    Optimizer space used: input 9/4500, output 4/3500
    4 table entries, 0 zero
    maximum spread: 257, maximum offset: 257
```

We show the entire *y.output* file here, but only the first few lines of each state are of interest now. A more complete explanation of *y.output* will be provided in section 3.1.

   yacc adds the rule

```
$accept : expression $end
```

to the grammar and places its position marker, indicated by an underscore _ in the rule, just before the start symbol, i.e., expression in this case. This is termed state 0. *yacc* then tries to move the position marker across the start symbol.

Whenever the position marker is located before a non-terminal, the position marker is placed before all of its formulations in parallel. A *state* is a set of formulations with position marked, which is derived in this fashion. A formulation together with the position mark is called a *configuration*.

A new state is computed as follows: for each configuration in the old state in turn, the position marker is moved across the next symbol. Within the old state, this is done for all configurations with the same next symbol in parallel. For each possible symbol, we thus reach a new set of configurations, termed a new state.

As described above, if the position marker in a configuration precedes a non-terminal symbol, all formulations for that symbol must be added to the state, with the position marker at the beginning of each new formulation.

The procedure must terminate, since there is by definition a finite number of rules and non-terminals, of formulations, and of terminals in a grammar, and since the formulations must be of finite length. The set of states is thus finite.

In the example, state 0 is constructed implicitly by *yacc*. Since the position marker precedes the non-terminal expression, we must add all formulations for it with the position marker at the beginning of each formulation:

```
expression : _expression - IDENTIFIER
expression : _IDENTIFIER
```

This is omitted in *y.output*, since it is obvious from the point of view of the *yacc* algorithm.

In the state, the position marker precedes expression and IDENTIFIER. Moving it across expression in all possible configurations, we obtain state 1; moving it across IDENTIFIER, we obtain state 2. In neither state the position marker precedes a non-terminal, and no new configurations result. State 2 only contains a *complete configuration*, where the position marker has reached the end of a formulation.

In state 1 we can move the position marker across the fictitious $end symbol added by *yacc*, and across the terminal − symbol in the other configuration. The former operation is essentially ignored; the latter produces state 3.

Again, state 3 cannot be extended, and we can only move the position marker across IDENTIFIER to reach state 4. This is the last possible state, since its only configuration is complete.

The algorithm just described is, of course, the simulation of using all parts of the grammar for input recognition. Moving the position marker across a terminal, a *shift* action, means to accept the terminal at a certain position in an input sequence; moving across a non-terminal symbol implies that a formulation for the non-terminal symbol has been completed elsewhere in the simulation. (This is discussed in more detail in chapter 3.)

The comments following the configurations in each state in *y.output* outline what actions would be taken during recognition for each possible input symbol. A period stands for *any other symbol* and reduce indicates the fact that a complete configuration, i.e., a certain formulation, would be used to collect a number of accepted symbols and to replace them by the appropriate non-terminal. reduce is accompanied by the number of the formulation to be used. shift indicates the next state which will be entered upon accepting the respective symbol.

1.5 Common pitfalls

It looks like nothing can go wrong in this analysis, but this is not the case. Forgetting to define terminal symbols, forgetting to define a rule for a non-terminal, or adding non-terminals and rules inaccessible from the start symbol are obvious errors, which *yacc* will discover and report immediately.

Problems with the grammar are more subtle and need individual attention. Consider the following excerpt dealing with the usual `if` statement:

```
/*
 *      dangling else
 */

%token  IF...THEN
%token  ELSE

%%

statement
        : ';'                   /* empty */
        | IF...THEN statement
        | IF...THEN statement ELSE statement
```

yacc will complain about a *shift/reduce conflict* and if we look at *y.output*, we find the following:

```
4: shift/reduce conflict (shift 5, red'n 2) on ELSE
state 4
        statement :  IF...THEN statement_     (2)
        statement :  IF...THEN statement_ELSE statement

        ELSE  shift 5
        .  reduce 2


state 5
        statement :  IF...THEN statement ELSE_statement

        IF...THEN  shift 3
        ;  shift 2
        .  error

        statement  goto 6
```

The problem is quite common. It concerns the question to which `if` the `else` belongs in the following program fragment:

```
if (condition)
        if (condition)
                ;                       /* empty statement */
        else
                ...
```

In terms of *yacc*, in state 4 we could still accept (shift) the terminal symbol ELSE and move on in the second configuration, or we could consider the first, complete configuration and substitute the non-terminal (reduce) statement. Shifting means to extend the innermost if statement, i.e., to connect each else to the innermost if, and this is what languages like C and Pascal require.

Technically, state 4 exhibits a shift/reduce conflict, a mistake in the proposed grammar, which makes it ambiguous and thus unsuitable for language recognition. *yacc*, however, intentionally permits such conflicts, and (as the comments indicate) it will provide for the longest possible input sequence, i.e., it will do just what is normally required.

The next problem is more serious. The setting is an excerpt from a Basic dialect, where the result of a comparison can be assigned to a variable or used in a decision:

```
/*
 *      multiple clauses
 */

%token  IDENTIFIER, IF, THEN, SUM

%%

statement
        : IDENTIFIER '=' expression
        | IF condition THEN statement

condition
        : expression
        | SUM '<' SUM

expression
        : SUM '<' SUM
        | SUM
```

yacc will note a *reduce/reduce conflict*, and investigation of *y.output* reveals the following:

```
state 14
        condition :  SUM < SUM_      (4)
        expression : SUM < SUM_      (5)

        .  reduce 4
```

State 14 contains more than one complete configuration. In this case, *yacc* would use the formulation introduced first in the grammar, but this tends to be risky if the grammar is later modified or rearranged. While we usually tolerate shift/reduce conflicts such as the dangling else problem, we always attempt to rewrite the grammar to eliminate formulation combinations which provoke reduce/reduce conflicts. In the present case this is easy — admittedly, the example is too simple to be realistic:

```
/*
 *      multiple clauses, no conflicts
 */
```

```
%token  IDENTIFIER, IF, THEN, SUM

%%

statement
        : IDENTIFIER '=' expression
        | IF expression THEN statement

expression
        : SUM '<' SUM
        | SUM
```

yacc has a very permissive syntax for its own input. For typographical reasons, we have even omitted the semicolon which may follow each rule. The inadvertent addition of an empty formulation can provoke a rather startling number of conflicts!

Another ambiguity problem is, in fact, a virtue. Consider the following grammar for arithmetic expressions:

```
expression
        : expression '+' expression
        | expression '-' expression
        | expression '*' expression
        | expression '/' expression
        | IDENTIFIER
```

While the description is short and devoid of extraneous non-terminal symbols, it does not convey any notions of precedence and associativity of the operators. *yacc* permits such a situation, as long as precedence and associativity are specified explicitly in the first part of the input file as follows:

```
%token  IDENTIFIER

%left   '+' '-'
%left   '*' '/'

%%
```

left defines a list of terminal symbols to be left-associative and to have equal precedence among each other. Precedence then increases in the order of appearance of successive left, right, and nonassoc lines in the input file. right, of course, indicates right-associativity, and nonassoc lists terminal symbols of equal precedence and does not permit them to associate with themselves.

This variety of ambiguity and explicit disambiguating rules is preferred — it introduces fewer non-terminals and thus streamlines a grammar.

1.6 Example

This book will show a complete compiler for *sampleC*, a rudimentary subset of C. The various modules for this compiler will be described in an "example" section near the end of each chapter.

Here is our informal definition of *sampleC* in extended BNF, where we enclose terminal symbols composed from special characters in quotes and specify reserved words in capital letters. Identifier and Constant are additional terminal symbols; unlike

the others, they stand for classes of words and not for themselves. The definition is
slightly verbose to simplify extensions left as exercises.

```
program
        : definition { definition }

definition
        : data_definition
        | function_definition

data_definition
        : INT declarator { ',' declarator } ';'

declarator
        : Identifier

function_definition
        : [ INT ] function_header function_body

function_header
        : declarator parameter_list

parameter_list
        : '(' [ Identifier_list ] ')' { parameter_declaration }

Identifier_list
        : Identifier { ',' Identifier }

parameter_declaration
        : INT declarator { ',' declarator } ';'

function_body
        : '{' { data_definition } { statement } '}'

statement
        : [ expression ] ';'
        | '{' { data_definition } { statement } '}'
        | IF '(' expression ')' statement [ ELSE statement ]
        | WHILE '(' expression ')' statement
        | BREAK ';'
        | CONTINUE ';'
        | RETURN [ expression ] ';'

expression
        : binary { ',' binary }

binary
        : Identifier '=' binary              from right
        | Identifier '+=' binary
        | Identifier '-=' binary
        | Identifier '*=' binary
        | Identifier '/=' binary
        | Identifier '%=' binary
        | binary '==' binary    precedence   from left
        | binary '!=' binary
        | binary '<' binary     precedence
```

```
                | binary '<=' binary
                | binary '>' binary
                | binary '>=' binary
                | binary '+' binary       precedence
                | binary '-' binary
                | binary '*' binary       precedence
                | binary '/' binary
                | binary '%' binary
                | unary

        unary
                : '++' Identifier
                | '--' Identifier
                | primary

        primary
                : Identifier
                | Constant
                | '(' expression ')'
                | Identifier '(' [ argument_list ] ')'

        argument_list
                : binary { ',' binary }
```

The semantics of *sampleC* are those of C, suitably pruned. The language has only an int data type, functions with a variable and arbitrary number of parameters and with int result, global, function-local and block-local scalar variables, and the control structures if-else and while. A number of the C operators are supported. Only one file will be compiled at a time, and a main() function must be present. This last condition will have to be explicitly accounted for; see chapter 5.

The informal definition above was translated into BNF. This involved mostly elaborating the repetitive constructs using recursion. A list of %token definitions and precedence relationships had to be added. The following result is acceptable to *yacc*:

```
        /*
         *      sample c
         *      syntax analysis
         *      (s/r conflict: one on ELSE)
         */

        /*
         *      terminal symbols
         */

        %token  Identifier
        %token  Constant
        %token  INT
        %token  IF
        %token  ELSE
        %token  WHILE
        %token  BREAK
        %token  CONTINUE
        %token  RETURN
        %token  ';'
        %token  '('
```

```
        %token  ')'
        %token  '{'
        %token  '}'
        %token  '+'
        %token  '-'
        %token  '*'
        %token  '/'
        %token  '%'
        %token  '>'
        %token  '<'
        %token  GE       /* >= */
        %token  LE       /* <= */
        %token  EQ       /* == */
        %token  NE       /* != */
        %token  '&'
        %token  '^'
        %token  '|'
        %token  '='
        %token  PE       /* += */
        %token  ME       /* -= */
        %token  TE       /* *= */
        %token  DE       /* /= */
        %token  RE       /* %= */
        %token  PP       /* ++
        %token  MM       /* -- */
        %token  ','

        /*
         *      precedence table
         */

        %right  '=' PE ME TE DE RE
        %left   '|'
        %left   '^'
        %left   '&'
        %left   EQ NE
        %left   '<' '>' GE LE
        %left   '+' '-'
        %left   '*' '/' '%'
        %right  PP MM

        %%

program
        : definitions

definitions
        : definition
        | definitions definition

definition
        : function_definition
        | INT function_definition
        | declaration

function_definition
```

```
                    : Identifier '(' optional_parameter_list ')'
                      parameter_declarations compound_statement

       optional_parameter_list
                    : /* no formal parameters */
                    | parameter_list

       parameter_list
                    : Identifier
                    | parameter_list ',' Identifier

       parameter_declarations
                    : /* null */
                    | parameter_declarations parameter_declaration

       parameter_declaration
                    : INT parameter_declarator_list ';'

       parameter_declarator_list
                    : Identifier
                    | parameter_declarator_list ',' Identifier

       compound_statement
                    : '{' declarations statements '}'

       declarations
                    : /* null */
                    | declarations declaration

       declaration
                    : INT declarator_list ';'

       declarator_list
                    : Identifier
                    | declarator_list ',' Identifier

       statements
                    : /* null */
                    | statements statement

       statement
                    : expression ';'
                    | ';'    /* null statement */
                    | BREAK ';'
                    | CONTINUE ';'
                    | RETURN ';'
                    | RETURN expression ';'
                    | compound_statement
                    | if_prefix statement
                    | if_prefix statement ELSE statement
                    | loop_prefix statement

       if_prefix
                    : IF '(' expression ')'

       loop_prefix
```

```
        : WHILE '(' expression ')'

expression
        : binary
        | expression ',' binary

binary
        : Identifier
        | Constant
        | '(' expression ')'
        | Identifier '(' optional_argument_list ')'
        | PP Identifier
        | MM Identifier
        | binary '+' binary
        | binary '-' binary
        | binary '*' binary
        | binary '/' binary
        | binary '%' binary
        | binary '>' binary
        | binary '<' binary
        | binary GE binary
        | binary LE binary
        | binary EQ binary
        | binary NE binary
        | binary '&' binary
        | binary '^' binary
        | binary '|' binary
        | Identifier '=' binary
        | Identifier PE binary
        | Identifier ME binary
        | Identifier TE binary
        | Identifier DE binary
        | Identifier RE binary

optional_argument_list
        : /* no actual arguments */
        | argument_list

argument_list
        : binary
        | argument_list ',' binary
```

1.7 A note on typography

As we remarked before, *yacc* input is almost entirely free format, but certain conventions are helpful:

Each nonterminal should appear just once on the left hand side of a rule. We place the nonterminal alone on a line, at the left margin. All formulations are then listed together.

The colon between left-hand and right-hand side of a rule is indented one tab position, the first formulation is indented one blank past the colon, and actions — to be discussed in chapter 3 — will be indented two tab positions.

The colon, the | symbol introducing an alternative formulation, and the semicolon terminating the rule are all vertically aligned.

In order to conserve space in the book, we do not terminate a rule by a semicolon. While this is acceptable to *yacc*, it is, however, a bad idea in practice to omit the semicolon, since omitting it tends to obscure typographical errors such as replacing a colon by a bar.

Rules are separated from one another by a blank line.

Empty formulations are clearly indicated by a suitable comment — this is particularly helpful for debugging.

We prefer long names, joined together by underscores; periods are also acceptable for this purpose. We also tend to use the suffix _list to indicate a comma-separated list of things, and plural to indicate a sequence of things.

1.8 Problems

1. Design a *small* subset of Pascal, and write a BNF description of it. Add token definitions and precedence relations to the BNF description. Submit this language definition to *yacc*, and correct it if necessary until is acceptable to *yacc* (i.e., until *yacc* does not issue any error messages other than unavoidable shift/reduce conflicts).

2. Extend the definition of *sampleC* by adding another standard feature of C, such as arrays. Change the grammar given in section 1.6 so that the new description of *sampleC* is acceptable to *yacc*.

3. Write a grammar for EBNF in BNF. A grammar for EBNF in EBNF can be found in section 1.2. What changes must be made to convert this grammar to BNF? Add token definitions and whatever else is needed to make the resulting grammar acceptable to *yacc*. Hint: to remove all shift/reduce conflicts, you will want to include a semicolon to terminate each rule.

2.1 Purpose

We have seen in the previous chapter that a language is a set of sentences, which in turn are sequences of terminal symbols. Terminal symbols in a programming language usually come in three varieties: operators are represented as (short) sequences of special characters, reserved words are represented as predefined sequences of letters whose meaning cannot vary, and user-defined terminal symbols encompass constants and identifiers subject to a specialized syntax definition. Then, of course, there is white space — blanks, tab characters and line separators — which in most modern programming languages merely separates terminal symbols but is otherwise insignificant. Comments, too, follow their own syntax, different for just about every programming language [Wic73] and just as insignificant as white space.

This chapter deals with *lexical analysis*, that phase of the compilation process which assembles terminal symbols from the unstructured sequence of input characters presented to the compiler. White space and comments are usually ignored, while operators and reserved words are identified and passed on using an internal representation — typically small integer constants. User-defined constants and identifiers need to be saved in an appropriate table, and a generic representation such as `Identifier` or `Constant` together with a reference to the table entry passed on.

We could attempt to solve the lexical analysis problem simultaneously with the actual language definition in the following manner:

```
statement
      : 'I' 'F' condition 'T' 'H' 'E' 'N' statement
```

The resulting grammar, however, is bound to be loaded with conflicts and the technique is horribly inefficient.

Lexical analysis accounts for a large amount of the processing which a real compiler does. By dealing with lexical analysis mostly independently from the rest of the compilation process, we can employ more appropriate techniques and can at the same time hide within a single module all knowledge about the actual representation of our programming language in a real world character set.

2.2 Definition tools

How *do* we assemble characters into terminal symbols? Lexical analysis is the classical application for the theory of finite state automata. A transition diagram is generally easy to devise from the lexical specification of a programming language, and an eight to sixteen hour *ad-hack* approach loosely based on the transition diagram will cope with just about any such specification. Things usually get messy when we need to dispose of strings, comments, and (floating-point) constants, in about that order. By way of illustration, let us consider a C-style comment described as a transition diagram:

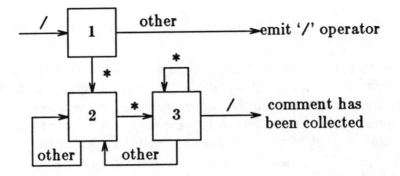

In a transition diagram, the states are the numbered nodes, and the transitions are the branches between the states, labeled with the input characters causing the transition. Characteristically, the exit from the diagram with the collected terminal symbol is somewhat haphazard — sometimes the following character has already been seen, and sometimes it has not.

A transition diagram corresponds quite closely to a syntax graph. The branches in the transition diagram describe the transitions; the nodes in the syntax graph contain the symbols which need to be found in order to move on. The difference is that syntax graphs regularly call one another, while these simple transition diagrams are not supposed to.

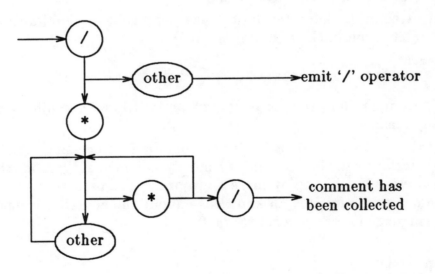

A comparison of the two types of diagrams suggests why transition diagrams are preferred in this approach to lexical analysis. The approach itself, however, is error prone, and the result tends to be quite hard to modify.

A better solution for the problem of lexical analysis can be derived directly from the theory: we need a convenient way to describe the finite state automaton corresponding to the lexical specification of our language, we need a compiler to produce appropriate tables from the description, and we need an interpreter to simulate the finite state automaton defined by the tables.

Such a compiler has, in fact, been written: it is called *lex* [Les78b]. *lex* accepts a table of patterns resembling editor patterns[1] and produces a table-driven C program

---

[1] See ed(1) in [Ker78a].

capable of recognizing input strings satisfying the patterns. As the *substitute* command in the editor shows, patterns can be conveniently used to identify specific character sequences.

Patterns are a very convenient specification language for the finite state automaton actually constructed. With each pattern a C statement can be associated which will be executed when a string satisfying the pattern is found in the input. In simple translation applications the C statement will usually write a modified copy of the string to standard output; in compiler applications the C statement should return an appropriate encoding of the string to the caller of the lexical analysis function.

As we shall see, *lex* is a very powerful tool in its own right, and it can be used to great advantage in language recognition. However, *lex* is, in our opinion, quite unfriendly to use: error messages are short and entirely unspecific, commenting input for *lex* is cumbersome at best, and brute force uses of *lex* can create huge programs. Still, *lex* is the tool of choice, since the alternative — hand-coding the lexical analysis function — requires a significantly higher investment in manpower.

The rest of this chapter will introduce in reasonable detail a sufficient number of *lex* features to cope with most compiler applications. We will first describe the most frequently used operations in patterns, how patterns are specified to *lex*, and how typical language constructs such as identifiers, strings, and comments can be specified as patterns. While we explain most possibilities, the chapter is not intended as a comprehensive description.

In section 2.5 we introduce *lex* as a program generator and we show a few small but complete *lex* programs for file inclusion, file splitting, and word counting. Our *sampleC* implementation is continued in section 2.7 where the complete lexical analyzer for *sampleC* is presented.

2.3 Patterns

Users of *ed* and similar text editors are already familiar with the following constituents of patterns:

Letters, digits, and some special characters represent themselves.

Period represents any character, with the exception of line feed.

Brackets, [and], enclose a sequence of characters, which is termed a *character class*. The class represents any one of its constituents, or any single character *not* in the given sequence if the sequence starts with ^. Within the sequence, — between two characters denotes the inclusive range.

If * follows one of these pattern parts, it indicates that the corresponding input may appear arbitrarily often, or even not at all.

^ at the beginning of a pattern represents the beginning of an input line.

$ at the end of a pattern represents the end of an input line (but not the line feed character itself).

With a suitable escape convention for special characters and white space, we can already write patterns for most terminal symbols of a programming language. There are two escape conventions in *lex*:

\ quotes a single following special character; in particular, two \ characters represent a single \. \ may precede the letters b, n, and t; the combinations then denote backspace, line feed, and tab characters, just as in C.

A better technique, especially for sequences of characters, is to enclose one or more characters in double-quotes. The characters thus lose their special meaning.

Most special characters have a special meaning in *lex*; if a special character should represent itself, it is best quoted. Special characters need not be quoted inside a character class. White space must always be quoted or represented by a \ escape sequence. A double-quote can be introduced within double-quotes with \", just as in C.

By way of example, let us look at patterns for some terminal symbols in *sampleC*. The operators are simply quoted — we generally prefer double-quotes to the backslash convention:

```
"*"
"--"
"*="
```

and so on. We need a pattern to recognize white space:

```
[ \t\n]
```

Constants consist of one or more digits:

```
[0-9][0-9]*
```

Identifiers follow the rules of C, i.e., they start in a letter or underscore and continue with arbitrarily many letters, digits, or underscores:

```
[A-Za-z_][A-Za-z0-9_]*
```

The following pattern attempts to deal with single-line comments:

```
"/*".*"*/"
```

A comment should start in /* and terminate with the *first* occurrence of */. It can extend over many lines.

The last two patterns exhibit certain limitations with which casual users of *ed* should be quite familiar: a pattern, by definition, represents the *longest* possible input sequence. In the case of constants and identifiers, this is really what is desired; in the case of comments, however, we need exactly the opposite! There is also a question as to what happens if we specify

```
"<"
"<="
```

i.e., two patterns which represent the same initial sequence of characters, or

```
"int"
[a-z][a-z]*
```

i.e., two patterns where one represents a subset of the possibilities of the other. We will deal with ambiguities in the next section.

In order to deal successfully with C- and Pascal-style comments and strings, we need to introduce a few more *lex* pattern features. Just as for *egrep*[2] parentheses may

---

[2] See grep(1) in [Ker78a].

be used for grouping within a pattern, | denotes alternatives, + denotes one or more occurrences of the item preceding it, and ? denotes zero or one occurrence. The last two features simplify some of the patterns shown earlier, e.g., integer constants are recognized with

    [0-9]+

A terminal symbol which is delimited by single characters, such as a Pascal-style comment enclosed in braces, is easy to handle:

    "{"[^}]*"}"

Using an alternative, the technique extends easily to Pascal- or C-style strings, where the delimiter must be duplicated or escaped if it is to appear within the string:

    \'([^'\n]|\'\')+\'
    \"([^"\n]|\\["\n])*\"

Note that a Pascal-style string as defined here cannot extend over several lines, and that it must contain at least one character. A C string can extend over several lines if the line feed is escaped using \, it can contain escaped double-quotes, and it can be empty.

If there is a sequence of characters used as a delimiter, as in C-style comments enclosed by /* and */, or in Pascal-style comments enclosed by (* and *), the necessary pattern becomes quite complicated. The basic idea is not to permit the terminating delimiter once the opening delimiter has been recognized; unfortunately, this can only be done by enumeration. Consider the following proposal for a pattern to recognize a C-style comment:

    "/*"([^*/]|[^*]"/"|"*"[^/])*"*/"

The comment begins with /* and ends with */. In between can be zero or more occurrences of one of three alternatives, namely any character but * or /, a / preceded by any character except *, or finally a * followed by any character other then /. Note that a character class using the complement operator ^ is somewhat dangerous — it usually includes line feed and thus can easily swallow an entire input file!

Alas, our 'solution' for C-style comments is not quite perfect: /*/ is not recognized as the beginning of a comment, since in this pattern, / must *follow* a character in the comment, and /***/ is not recognized as a complete comment, since in this pattern * must *precede* another character in the comment, which causes the third * to be ignored as part of the delimiter. A better solution is the following pattern, which admittedly is even harder to read:

    "/*""/"*([^*/]|[^*]"/"|"*"[^/])*"*"*"*"*/"

Now zero or more slashes may immediately follow the opening delimiter, and zero or more asterisks may precede the closing delimiter. Thus the special cases are also accounted for.

There is yet more to *lex* patterns. Iteration can be limited to a specific range using a notation like

    [a-z][a-z0-9]{0,7}

to denote an identifier starting in a lower case letter, which is followed by zero to seven letters or digits. A pattern may be recognized only before a certain right context, which itself is not represented by the pattern; the right context is given following a / mark:

```
-0[xX]/[0-9a-f]+
```

would recognize the sign and the base prefix of a negative hexadecimal C constant, but would not include the digits of the constant itself. Patterns can be preceded by start conditions, which essentially permit the dynamic selection of one of several sets of patterns specified together. Finally, a very able (and careful) programmer can even interact directly with the input, output, and buffer managing routines employed by the automaton generated by *lex*. The patient and imaginative reader is cheerfully referred to the original publication [Les78b].

2.4 Ambiguity as a virtue

A set of *lex* patterns tends to be highly ambiguous. Two rules are employed by *lex* to sort things out:

lex always chooses that pattern which represents the longest possible input string.

If two patterns represent the same string, the first pattern in the list presented to *lex* is chosen.

Both rules are, in fact, assets rather than liabilities. The first rule asserts that the patterns

```
int
[a-z]+
```

completely recognize integer (as an instance of the second pattern) and not only the initial int. The second rule causes the pattern int and not the second, more general pattern to recognize int from the input.

As has been demonstrated in the previous section, the first disambiguating rule can backfire if used carelessly. The second rule, however, encourages an arrangement in which the most general pattern, e.g., for an identifier, is placed last, with more selective patterns preceding it to pick off exceptions.

Consider the following recognition problem: when typing German texts on an American keyboard, *umlaut* characters are most quickly typed as ae, oe, ue, etc. Before the resulting document is presented to *nroff* or *troff* to be processed, e.g., with the *ms* macro package [Les78a], one should replace all these letter combinations by invocations of the *ms* string *:, as for example in *:a, *:o, etc. The pattern

```
ue
```

however, recognizes the letter combination ue even in contexts such as Quelle (German: fountain), or eventuell (German: possibly), where it does not represent the umlaut. We therefore need to pick off these special cases *before* we present the general combination:

```
[Qq]ue
ntue
ue
```

Since ambiguous pattern lists are acceptable as input to *lex*, we can simply insert more special cases as we encounter them.

Unlike in *yacc*, where only in the case of reduce/reduce conflicts does input order make a difference, it greatly matters in *lex* since conflicts in the sense of *yacc* are frequently encountered. This, unfortunately, often leads to illogical arrangements of the patterns. The order of patterns does imply something like a control structure.

2.5 "lex" programs

Input to *lex* consists of one file with three parts, separated by lines beginning in %%:

```
    first part

    %%

    pattern         action
              . . .

    %%

    third part
```

The first part is optional; it can contain lines controlling the dimensions of certain tables internal to *lex*, it can contain definitions for text replacements as we shall see in section 2.7, and it can contain (global) C code preceded by a line beginning in %{ and followed by a line beginning in %}. Even if the first part of the *lex* specification is empty, the separator %% between the first and second parts of the *lex* specification cannot be omitted.

The third part and the separator preceding it are optional. The third part contains C code which is used as is. As we shall see, it usually contains (local) functions which the second part uses.

The second part of the specification consists of a table of patterns and actions. This part of the specification is quite line-oriented. A pattern starts at the beginning of a line and extends to the first non-escaped white space. Following an arbitrary amount of white space, an action is specified which is thus associated with the pattern. The action is a single C statement, or several statements enclosed in a set of braces. The action may also consist of a bar |, indicating that the present pattern will use the same action as the next pattern.

lex input itself has no provisions for comments(!), but within braces, regular C comments can be written.

From the table, *lex* will construct a C function yylex() in the file *lex.yy.c*. If this function is linked with a program and called, standard input is read until the next, longest possible string represented by a pattern has been collected. The action associated with the pattern is then executed. If this action contains a return statement, yylex() will return, possibly with a function value as dictated by the return statement.

lex adds a default pattern and action to the patterns specified by the user in such a way that all otherwise unrecognized input characters are copied to standard output.

The following *lex* program will remove all upper case letters from its input:

```
%{
/*
 *      remove upper case letters
 */
%}

%%

[A-Z]+
```

Assuming that the program is contained in a file *exuc.l*, the following commands produce an executable program *exuc*:

```
lex exuc.l
cc lex.yy.c -ll -o exuc
```

-ll references the *lex* library, which contains a default `main()` function, which will just call `yylex()` once. This library must always be supplied when a function `yylex()` generated by *lex* is to be linked.

More useful actions need to have access to the input string recognized by the pattern with which they are associated. The char vector `yytext[]` contains this string, null-terminated, the int variable `yyleng` has `strlen(yytext)` as a value, and the int variable `yylineno` contains the number of the current input line. Let us look at a few marginally useful programs:

```
%{
/*
 *      line numbering
 */
%}

%%

\n       ECHO;
^.*$     printf("%d\t%s", yylineno, yytext);
```

This first program prints standard input and precedes each nonempty input line by its number and a tab character. ECHO is defined within the C program produced by *lex*; it causes `yytext[]` to be printed.

If we also want to number the empty lines, the following program can be used:

```
%{
/*
 *      line numbering
 */
%}

%%

^.*\n    printf("%d\t%s", yylineno-1, yytext);
```

Now we recognize line feed as part of the pattern. `yylineno` is already incremented to the next line when our action gets control.

The next program is an author's favorite utility:

```
%{
/*
 *      word count
 */

int     nchar, nword, nline;
%}

%%

\n              ++ nchar, ++ nline;
[^ \t\n]+       ++ nword, nchar += yyleng;
.                 ++ nchar;

%%

main()
{
        yylex();
        printf("%d\t%d\t%d\n", nchar, nword, nline);
}
```

This example shows a use for the third part of a *lex* specification: we include our own `main()` function, which here prints the statistics gathered during execution of the `yylex()` function.

The next example is typical of a large class of problems, where a special action — here it is file inclusion — needs to be taken when just one pattern is recognized. Most of the input is just passed through. Similar applications include, e.g., adorning reserved words for the publication of a program, gathering a table of contents, etc.

```
%{
/*
 *      .so filename    file inclusion
 */

#include <ctype.h>
#include <stdio.h>

static include();
%}

%%

^".so".*\n      { yytext[yyleng-1] = '\0'; include(yytext+3); }

%%

static include(s)
        char * s;
{       FILE * fp;
        int i;

        while (*s && isspace(*s))
```

```
                        ++ s;
            if (fp = fopen(s, "r"))
            {       while ((i = getc(fp)) != EOF)
                            output(i);
                    fclose(fp);
            }
            else
                    perror(s);
    }
```

output() is the routine which *lex* uses to write all output. The program can only handle one level of file inclusion.

The last example deals with depositing output in several files, selected by options in the input. This is a variant of the *split* utility.

```
    %{
    /*
     *          .di filename      file splitting
     */

    #include <ctype.h>
    #include <stdio.h>
    static divert();
    %}

    %%

    ^".di".*\n          { yytext[yyleng-1] = '\0'; divert(yytext+3); }

    %%

    static divert(s)
            char * s;
    {
            while (*s && isspace(*s))
                    ++ s;
            if (! freopen(s, "w", stdout))
                    perror(s);
    }
```

This example is quite difficult to handle with tools such as *sed* or *awk*, where the number of output files is severely limited. Since *lex* can pick the file name from within a complex context, this solution is significantly easier to modify than a hand-written C program.

2.6 Testing a lexical analyzer

For use as a lexical analyzer in a compiler, yylex() should be designed as a function returning an int value. Upon each call, the next terminal symbol should be collected from the input, encoded, and returned as the function value. Each pattern now is designed to recognize one or more terminal symbols, and the associated action will contain a return statement to produce the function value. We must make provisions so that *all* input characters are recognized, even if they neither belong to terminal symbols, nor are to be ignored silently, since yylex() is supposed to let all input disappear in this case.

Testing such a function can be messy — the function values are numbers and as such usually not terribly mnemonic. We found a C programming trick quite helpful.[3] For debugging purposes we arrange for the *lex* program to have the following principal architecture:

```
%{
#include <assert.h>
#define token(x)        (int) "x"
main()
{       char * p;

        assert(sizeof(int) >= sizeof(char *));
        while (p = (char *) yylex())
                printf("%s is \"%s\"\n", p, yytext);
}
%}

%%

pattern         return token(MNEMONIC);
```

As the *sampleC* example will show, it is possible to build a lexical analyzer in such a way that it can always be conditionally compiled for testing purposes in this fashion.

The caller of yylex() receives the value MNEMONIC in printable form as a result value of yylex(). The simple main() routine will then display the input text yytext and a decoded representation of the returned value together for debugging purposes.

By convention, yylex() is expected to return zero(!) as an end of file indication. *lex* generates the function yylex() so that this happens internally; main() is coded to terminate once yylex() returns zero.

One last advice: the reserved words of a programming language are particularly easy to write down as patterns. Unfortunately, a long list of such self-representing patterns dramatically increases the size of the program generated by *lex*. It is much more efficient to collect reserved words and identifiers with the same, single pattern and to screen the results with a small C function. A standard approach to this problem is shown in the next section.

2.7 Example

From the *yacc* specification of *sampleC* we know which terminal symbols must be found by the lexical analysis routine for this compiler: yylex() needs to find all symbols mentioned in %token statements and all single-character terminal symbols quoted directly. At present, using the debugging technique introduced in the previous section, we do not need to worry about the exact function values which must be returned as encodings of the various terminal symbols.

---

[3] Unfortunately, this trick will not work on machines such as the MC 68000, where pointer values do not fit into int variables. The library macro assert() is employed to guard against this possibility; it will abort the program if the given condition is not met.

The patterns pose no problems, since we will eventually run the C preprocessor prior to our own compiler. The C preprocessor will remove comments(!), and it makes the usual #define, #include, and conditional compilation facilities available for our *sampleC* implementation.

The complete, final lexical analyzer is shown below. DEBUG must be defined when we compile the lexical analyzer for testing purposes. A few lines in the following file should therefore be ignored at present; they will be explained in chapter 3 where we integrate our language recognition program.

```
%{
/*
 *       sample c -- lexical analysis
 */

#ifdef  DEBUG           /* debugging version - if assert ok */

#       include <assert.h>

        main()
        {       char * p;

                assert(sizeof(int) >= sizeof(char *));

                while (p = (char *) yylex())
                        printf("%-10.10s is \"%s\"\n", p, yytext);
        }

        s_lookup() {}
        int yynerrs = 0;

#       define  token(x)        (int) "x"

#else   ! DEBUG         /* production version */

#       include "y.tab.h"
#       define  token(x)        x

#endif  DEBUG

#define END(v)  (v-1 + sizeof v / sizeof v[0])
static int screen();
%}

letter                  [a-zA-Z_]
digit                   [0-9]
letter_or_digit         [a-zA-Z_0-9]
white_space             [ \t\n]
blank                   [ \t]
other

%%

^"#"{blank}*{digit}+({blank}+.*)?\n     yymark();

">="                                    return token(GE);
```

```
"<="                               return token(LE);
"=="                               return token(EQ);
"!="                               return token(NE);
"+="                               return token(PE);
"-="                               return token(ME);
"*="                               return token(TE);
"/="                               return token(DE);
"%="                               return token(RE);
"++"                               return token(PP);
"--"                               return token(MM);

{letter}{letter_or_digit}*         return screen();

{digit}+                           { s_lookup(token(Constant));
                                     return token(Constant);
                                   }

{white_space}+

{other}                            return token(yytext[0]);

%%

/*
 *      reserved word screener
 */

static struct rwtable {            /* reserved word table */
        char * rw_name;            /* representation */
        int rw_yylex;             /* yylex() value */
        } rwtable[] = {            /* sorted */
        "break",          token(BREAK),
        "continue",       token(CONTINUE),
        "else",           token(ELSE),
        "if",             token(IF),
        "int",            token(INT),
        "return",         token(RETURN),
        "while",          token(WHILE),
        };

static int screen()
{       struct rwtable * low = rwtable,
                * high = END(rwtable),
                * mid;
        int c;

        while (low <= high)
        {       mid = low + (high-low)/2;
                if ((c = strcmp(mid->rw_name, yytext)) == 0)
                        return mid->rw_yylex;
                else if (c < 0)
                        low = mid+1;
                else
                        high = mid-1;
        }
        s_lookup(token(Identifier));
```

```
        return token(Identifier);
}
```

Assuming that this text is in the file *samplec.l*, the lexical analyzer is compiled for testing purposes as follows:

```
lex samplec.l
cc -DDEBUG lex.yy.c -ll -o lexi
```

We can run some tests through this lexical analyzer to check if the proper terminal symbols are recognized. The simplest, complete program is as follows:

```
main() {}
```

For this program the lexical analyzer will return the following:

```
Identifier is "main"
yytext[0]  is "("
yytext[0]  is ")"
yytext[0]  is "{"
yytext[0]  is "}"
```

We took a very simple approach to recognizing single character operators and at the same time finding and signaling all illegal input characters: if no other pattern catches a character, it is returned itself as value of yylex(). In this fashion we obtain a compact lexical analyzer, and we will later deal with all input errors in a systematic way.

A few other features of the lexical analyzer are perhaps worth mentioning. *lex* has a rudimentary text replacement facility within the patterns. A line of the form

```
    name    replacement
```

in the first part of the *lex* specification defines a replacement text for a name. The name can then be specified as

```
    {name}
```

within a pattern, and the replacement will be substituted. We use this facility often, usually to make the patterns more transparent and mnemonic.

The first pattern deals with lines of the form

```
# linenumber filename
```

Such lines are produced by the C preprocessor as position stamps during file inclusion and selection for conditional compilation. As will be explained in chapter 3, yymark() is a function which we designed to record the relevant information for our own error messages.

As promised, we use a simple binary lookup function screen() to recognize reserved words as special cases of those terminal symbols recognized by the identifier pattern. screen() is really intended as a blueprint solution for such a screening problem. Notice how the token technique is even used in the reserved word table!

s_lookup() is a handle for symbol table management which we will use and explain beginning in chapter 5.

2.8 Problems

1. Write a *lex* program which will read a Pascal program and print out only (* *) comments, eliminating everything else. Hint: what modifications are needed to the *lex* pattern for C comments given in section 2.3?

2. Write a *lex* pattern which will recognize a Fortran REAL constant, defined as a string of digits having either a decimal point or an E-type exponent, or both. For an additional challenge, take into account the fact that in Fortran, white space is allowed anywhere outside of quote marks, even within the characters of a constant, identifier, or keyword.

3. Using the pattern in problem 2, write a complete *lex* program which will read a Fortran program and convert all REAL constants to DOUBLE PRECISION. The program should also change all REAL variable declarations to DOUBLE PRECISION. (It is convenient that the word REAL occurs in Fortran only as a variable declaration statement, assuming that it is not foolishly used as a variable name.)

4. Write a complete *lex* program which will read a program written in your favorite programming language, recognize all of the keywords in that program, and print them in upper case letters. All other upper case letters should be converted to lower case. Hint: use a function like screen() (see section 2.7) to recognize the keywords.

5. Write a complete *lex* program which will read a program written in your favorite programming language and produce a cross-reference table of all identifiers in the program. Hint: once your *lex* program recognizes an identifier, it should use suitable C functions to compare it to a table of language keywords, which can be ignored, and to the list of other previously recognized identifiers. New identifiers should be added to the latter list. Each list entry should be the head of a chain of cross-reference elements which record values obtained from yylineno. After yylex() terminates, the cross-reference table can be printed.

Chapter 3
Language Recognition

In this chapter, we will be putting things together: a grammar presented to *yacc*, a lexical analyzer specification presented to *lex*, combined with a rudimentary symbol table facility, make up a language recognizer. As the example will show, such a recognizer can be used for such things as pretty-printing programs.

To start, we need to understand the workings of the *parser* which *yacc* constructs from a grammar, deposits in the file *y.tab.c*, and describes in the file *y.output*. With this background in place, we show in section 3.2 how a recognizer for *sampleC* is actually put together.

It turns out that we must supply a `main()` program to drive the recognizer and a procedure `yyerror()` which will be called from the parser if an error is discovered in the input. In section 3.3 we take time out to present a comfortable version of `main()` which allows us to optionally invoke the C preprocessor prior to our own compiler. We also construct a general `yyerror()` function which gives a clear indication of the position of an error in the input to the parser.

Unfortunately, grammars do not always immediately reflect the true intentions of the language designer. In section 3.4 we therefore discuss how one goes about finding bugs in the recognizer. It turns out that the file *y.output* and a debugging option provided by *yacc* can be combined into a useful strategy to locate "misunderstandings" in the grammar.

We will conclude the chapter with a formatter for *sampleC*. Before we can actually implement such a program, we must still solve the problem of passing information *about* terminal symbols from the lexical analyzer to the parser. Thus, in section 3.5, *actions* enter the picture in *yacc* specifications, and we demonstrate their flexibility by constructing a simple desk calculator.

3.1 Parser generation

We explained in section 1.4 how *yacc* analyzes a grammar. The analysis amounted to traversing all rules in a highly parallel fashion while simulating arbitrary terminal symbol acceptance. If we can somehow feed real input to this algorithm, things must actually get simpler: rather than following numerous possibilities in parallel, *yacc* can then move through only those states which are selected by the input. The result must be a device for language recognition, a *parser* or *syntax analyzer*.

yacc, in fact, builds a parser while analyzing the grammar. The parser is a push-down automaton — a stack machine — consisting of a "large" stack to hold current states, a transition matrix to derive a new state for each possible combination of current state and next input symbol, a table of user-definable actions which are to be executed at certain points in the recognition, and finally an interpreter to actually permit execution. The result is packaged as a function `yyparse()`, which calls repeatedly on a lexical analyzer function `yylex()` to read standard input, and which returns zero or one to indicate whether or not a sentence was presented as input file.

We can visualize the parser function as follows:

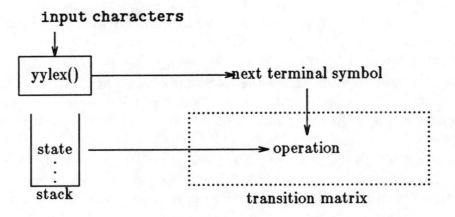

Current state, on top of the stack, and next terminal symbol, produced as needed by a call to yylex(), select an operation from the transition matrix. The file *y.output* shows the contents of the transition matrix for each acceptable next terminal symbol and each state. Five types of operations will be found in the transition matrix:

accept

This operation happens only once, namely when we have $end as next terminal symbol, represented as a non-positive value of yylex(), and are getting ready to successfully complete recognition.

error

This operation is found as element of the transition matrix for all those next terminal symbols which must not be seen in a particular current state.

shift *new state*

This operation indicates that the next terminal symbol is acceptable in the current state. The *new state* is pushed onto the stack and becomes the current state. We have, in fact, moved on in some configuration.

reduce *formulation number*

This operation is present in the transition matrix for all those states which contain a complete configuration. The *formulation number* indicates the complete configuration; it appears following the configuration in the file *y.output*. At this point, we will pop as many states off the stack as the formulation has symbols. The uncovered state on top of the stack is the new current state. The non-terminal whose formulation was just completed is used prior to the next terminal symbol. The actual next terminal symbol will be processed following the non-terminal symbol just explained.

goto *new state*

As we just saw, a reduce operation implicitly generates a non-terminal symbol to be used prior to the next terminal symbol. goto is the shift operation for this non-terminal symbol. A shift operation always uses and discards the next terminal symbol; a goto operation uses a non-terminal symbol and leaves the next terminal symbol for a subsequent shift operation. Otherwise, goto and shift operate in the same fashion: the *new state* is pushed onto the stack and becomes the current state.

To illustrate the operations in context, let us look again at the simple grammar introduced in chapter 1:

```
expression
        : expression '-' IDENTIFIER
        | IDENTIFIER
```

In chapter 1 we introduced a file *y.output* which *yacc* can produce from this grammar. We will now once again look at this file to demonstrate that it in fact fully documents the parser. The parser starts out with state 0 as current state on the stack:

```
state 0
        $accept : _expression $end

        IDENTIFIER  shift 2
           error

        expression  goto 1
```

If the next terminal symbol is an IDENTIFIER, we will perform a shift operation, i.e., we will accept the symbol and push the new current state 2 onto the stack. Any other input symbol would be considered in error.

```
state 2
        expression :  IDENTIFIER_      (2)

        . reduce 2
```

Without regard to the new next terminal symbol, we will use formulation 2 for a reduce operation, i.e., since formulation 2 consists of one symbol (IDENTIFIER), we will pop one state of the stack. Having come this far we uncover state 0.

The reduce operation has just generated expression as a non-terminal symbol, and the instructions for state 0 prescribe that we goto state 1 in this situation. Notice that the next terminal symbol, if any, has thus far not been considered.

```
state 1
        $accept :  expression_$end
        expression :  expression_- IDENTIFIER

        $end  accept
        -  shift 3
        .  error
```

In state 1 we consider the symbol following the first IDENTIFIER in the input. $end, the end of input, or a — operator are anticipated at this point. $end leads to an accept operation — our parser has recognized IDENTIFIER as a sentence! It would be instructive for the reader to follow the parser actions in *y.ouput* for a longer sentence.

One problem remains: how does yylex() know what values yyparse() expects as representations of the next terminal symbol? A natural convention is to represent single characters as terminal symbols by their value in the character set, i.e., the C constant 'x' will represent the terminal symbol 'x' in the grammar presented to *yacc*. For a terminal symbol name, introduced by a %token statement in *yacc*, however, yyparse() and yylex() must use the same integer value as a representation; this value must be distinguishable from the representation of single characters.

yacc aids in defining suitable values. The command

```
yacc -d grammar.y
```

instructs *yacc* to produce a file *y.tab.h* containing one C preprocessor #define statement for each name introduced as %token.[1] The replacement text for each name is a unique integer constant, starting at 257.

The file *y.tab.h* is already present within the file *y.tab.c*, which is also produced by *yacc*, and which contains the function yyparse(). The same terminal symbol representations can thus be used for yylex() by including *y.tab.h* with a C preprocessor #include statement in the definition of the lexical analysis function.

This requires, however, that names used in the grammar for terminal symbols and introduced through %token statements cannot be reserved words in C. The lexical analysis function yylex() can be written by hand, or it can be produced by *lex* as discussed in chapter 2.

3.2 Example

In section 1.6, we presented *sampleC* in a form acceptable to *yacc*. Assume that this definition is in a file *samplec.y*. In section 2.7, we showed the file *samplec.l* containing a lexical analyzer for the terminal symbols of *sampleC*. We can now put both functions together to obtain a parser for *sampleC*.

If we do *not* define DEBUG while compiling the lexical analyzer, the C preprocessor statements

```
#include "y.tab.h"
#define token(x) x
```

in *samplec.l* will take effect. The first causes the terminal symbol representations produced by *yacc* in *y.tab.h* to be used in compiling yylex(). The second statement disables our debugging technique for the lexical analyzer: for debugging, we returned the terminal symbol names via

```
#define token(x) int "x"
```

as printable C strings. Now we return the *values* for those names, as defined in *y.tab.h*.

The very last pattern in the lexical analyzer:

```
{other}          return token(yytext[0]);
```

takes care of returning the character values for all unrecognized single character terminal symbols. This pattern is placed last so that a single letter or digit is recognized by

---

[1] Terminal symbol names can also be introduced through a first appearance in %left, %right, or %nonassoc statements. We prefer to *always* define terminal symbols first with %token.

earlier patterns as an `Identifier` or a `Constant`.

We produce the recognizer with the following commands:

```
lex samplec.l
yacc -d samplec.y
cc lex.yy.c y.tab.c -ll
```

Actually — not quite. If we compile in this fashion, we pick the `main()` routine from the *lex* library, and as we saw in chapter 2, this routine will only call `yylex()` once and the parser `yyparse()` not at all! We need to supply a different `main()` routine such as

```
main()
{
        yyparse();
}
```

One more routine must also be provided by the user of *yacc*. When the parser executes an `error` operation in the transition matrix, there is a syntax error in the input file. At this point, an error message should be written, and `yyparse()` therefore issues the call

```
yyerror("syntax error");
```

It is up to us to program a suitable `yyerror()` routine indicating the input position, etc. A trivial solution is the following:

```
#include <stdio.h>

yyerror(s)
        char * s;
{
        fputs(s, stderr), putc('\n', stderr);
}
```

We need not count the individual errors. This is handled automatically by `yyparse()` in the `int` variable `yynerrs`.

If those two routines are in a file *extra.c*, we can complete the compilation begun above with the command

```
cc extra.c lex.yy.o y.tab.o -ll
```

The resulting recognizer in file *a.out* can be executed as follows:

```
a.out
main() { }
^D
```

Nothing happens, and this is as it should be:

```
main() { }
```

is a very small, legal *sampleC* program. Our recognizer will produce nothing at all if the input is in fact a sentence. If it is not, we will be faced by a curt `syntax error`.

3.3 Auxiliary functions

The `main()` and `yyerror()` routines shown in the preceding section are of the software engineering quality of *lex*. User-friendly compilers should pinpoint input errors at least at the line number level, and the error messages should be more than just syntax error. In this section we discuss a general approach to this problem.

We begin with the `main()` routine. It turns out that it is quite convenient to always be able to invoke the C preprocessor to obtain standard file inclusion, text replacement, and conditional compilation facilities. Also, the C preprocessor will remove C-style comments, unless the −C option is specified. Our standard `main()` routine will invoke the C preprocessor if at least one of the option arguments known to the preprocessor is used; we can thus always provoke preprocessing through the −P or −E option:

```
/*
 *      main() -- possibly run C preprocessor before yyparse()
 */

#include <stdio.h>

static usage(name)
        register char * name;
{
        fputs("usage: ", stderr);
        fputs(name, stderr);
        fputs(" [C preprocessor options] [source]\n", stderr);
        exit(1);
}

main(argc, argv)
        int argc;
        char ** argv;
{       char ** argp;
        int cppflag = 0;

        for (argp = argv; *++argp && **argp == '-'; )
                switch ((*argp)[1]) {
                default:
                        usage(argv[0]);
                case 'C':
                case 'D':
                case 'E':
                case 'I':
                case 'P':
                case 'U':
                        cppflag = 1;
                }
        if (argp[0] && argp[1])
                usage(argv[0]);
        if (*argp && ! freopen(*argp, "r", stdin))
                perror(*argp), exit(1);
        if (cppflag && cpp(argc, argv))
                perror("C preprocessor"), exit(1);
        exit(yyparse());
}
```

The routine checks all arguments. Options always start with −. If there is an option known to the C preprocessor, the preprocessor will be invoked through our function cpp() described below, which is given access to all the arguments. Following the options, there may be one file name argument, which will be opened as the source file. After argument processing, main() calls yyparse() and propagates the return value as exit() code of the process. As a test bed, this routine is quite convenient. When a compiler nears completion, the routine is usually extended with more option processing and usage information output for illegal arguments.

The routine cpp(), which actually runs the C preprocessor, is somewhat involved. An elegant solution which avoids having temporary files hinges upon being able to connect a pipeline so that yylex() is implicitly forced to read from it. By definition, yylex() reads single characters by calling a routine input() defined as a macro by *lex*. It turns out that this routine in turn reads from the file pointer yyin which is externally accessible. This can be used in cpp():

```
/*
 *      cpp() -- preprocess lex input() through C preprocessor
 */

#include <stdio.h>

#ifndef CPP                             /* filename of C preprocessor */
#       define   CPP      "/lib/cpp"
#endif

int cpp(argc, argv)
        int argc;
        char ** argv;
{       char ** argp, * cmd;
        extern FILE * yyin;     /* for lex input() */
        extern FILE * popen();
        int i;

        for (i = 0, argp = argv; *++argp; )
                if (**argp == '-' &&
                    index("CDEIUP", (*argp)[1]))
                        i += strlen(*argp) + 1;

        if (! (cmd = (char *) calloc(i + sizeof CPP, sizeof(char))))
                return -1;      /* no room */

        strcpy(cmd, CPP);
        for (argp = argv; *++argp; )
                if (**argp == '-' &&
                    index("CDEIPU", (*argp)[1]))
                        strcat(cmd, " "), strcat(cmd, *argp);

        if (yyin = popen(cmd, "r"))
                i = 0;          /* all's well */
        else
                i = -1;         /* no preprocessor */
        cfree(cmd);
        return i;
}
```

cpp() first measures the string length of all options known to the C preprocessor. It then acquires memory for a composite string and builds a command to call the C preprocessor with those options. Using popen() from the standard library, the C preprocessor is connected as a filter to yyin, the command string is freed, and cpp() returns zero if all this has worked.

Turning now to error reporting, we first present a standard header for messages giving a sensible amount of positioning information. We would like to include the name of the source file, especially when files are preprocessed by the C preprocessor. The current line number yylineno is maintained correctly by *lex* as long as no preprocessing takes place. The current or next token can be found in yytext[] but this token may be a line feed; at the end of the source file it might even be empty. In both cases, the actual line number of the error is less than yylineno. A lot of information can be provided in an automated fashion, but it needs to be carefully formatted:

```
/*
 *      yywhere() -- input position for yyparse()
 *      yymark() -- get information from '# line file'
 */

#include <stdio.h>

extern FILE * yyerfp;             /* error stream */

extern char yytext[];             /* current token */
extern int yyleng;                /* and its length */
extern int yylineno;              /* current input line number */

static char * source;             /* current input file name */

yywhere()                         /* position stamp */
{       char colon = 0;           /* a flag */

        if (source && *source && strcmp(source, "\"\""))
        {       char * cp = source;
                int len = strlen(source);

                if (*cp == '"')
                        ++cp, len -= 2;
                if (strncmp(cp, "./", 2) == 0)
                        cp += 2, len -= 2;
                fprintf(yyerfp, "file %.*s", len, cp);
                colon = 1;
        }
        if (yylineno > 0)
        {       if (colon)
                        fputs(", ", yyerfp);
                fprintf(yyerfp, "line %d",
                        yylineno -
                        (*yytext == '\n' || ! *yytext));
                colon = 1;
        }
        if (*yytext)
        {       register int 1;
```

```
                for (i = 0; i < 20; ++ i)
                        if (!yytext[i] || yytext[i] == '\n')
                                break;
                if (i)
                {       if (colon)
                                putc(' ', yyerfp);
                        fprintf(yyerfp, "near \"%.*s\"", i, yytext);
                        colon = 1;
                }
        }
        if (colon)
                fputs(": ", yyerfp);
}

yymark()                                /* retrieve from '# digits text' */
{
        if (source)
                cfree(source);
        source = (char *) calloc(yyleng, sizeof(char));
        if (source)
                sscanf(yytext, "# %d %s", &yylineno, source);
}
```

We define `yyerfp` as a separate file pointer, which is used for all messages. The compiler designer can thus still choose to emit the messages as standard output (the default), or to write them to a separate file simply by assigning a different file pointer to `yyerfp`.

`yymark()` is a routine which extracts source file and line information from the position stamps emitted by the C preprocessor; see section 2.7.

If all possible parts are present, the message header produced by `yywhere()` would appear as follows:

```
source.c, line 10 near "badsymbol":
```

where `badsymbol` usually is the symbol following the error.

We are now ready to write a standard `yyerror()` routine which better pinpoints the location of an error:

```
#include <stdio.h>

FILE * yyerfp = stdout;          /* error stream */

yyerror(s)
        register char * s;
{       extern int yynerrs;      /* total number of errors */

        fprintf(yyerfp, "[error %d] ", yynerrs+1);
        yywhere();
        fputs(s, yyerfp);
        putc('\n', yyerfp);
}
```

`yynerrs` is a counter which is maintained by *yacc*; this counter is incremented once after each call to `yyerror()` is issued. Especially in a long compilation protocol, it is quite helpful if the error messages are sequentially numbered.

3.4 Debugging the parser

The parser is ready for testing. Unfortunately, nothing at all will happen if we present a correct input file to our parser for processing. If the input file is incorrect, we will receive one more or less useful error message. If we believe that the input file is correct, but the error message appears anyhow, things can get messy: we need to discover why yyparse() decided to issue a call to the error message routine.

The technique outlined in section 2.6 enables us to verify that the lexical analyzer is not at fault, i.e., that yyparse() actually received the symbols which we assume to be in the input file. Once this has been verified, we can use a debugging facility provided by *yacc*: if we compile the parser *y.tab.c* with the symbol YYDEBUG defined

```
cc -DYYDEBUG y.tab.c lex.yy.c main.c yyerror.c -ll
```

the resulting yyparse() function contains a tracing option which can be enabled by setting the int variable yydebug to a nonzero value. yydebug is a global variable and can for example be set with *adb*:

```
adb -w a.out
yydebug?w 1
$q
```

We illustrate the results of tracing with slightly modified versions of the simple expression grammar introduced in section 1.4. Here is a rudimentary lexical analyzer:

```
%{
#include "y.tab.h"
%}
%%

[a-z]+              return IDENTIFIER;
[ \t\n]+            ;
                    return yytext[0];
```

The first version of the grammar defines − to be left-associative as a disambiguating rule:

```
%token  IDENTIFIER
%left   '-'
%%

expression
        : expression '-' expression
        | IDENTIFIER

%%

main()
{
#ifdef  YYDEBUG
        extern int yydebug;

        yydebug = 1;
```

```
        #endif
                printf("yyparse() == %d\n", yyparse());
        }
```

Just like a *lex* specification, the input file for *yacc* may also contain a third part preceded by %%. This part is copied into *y.tab.c*; here it contains a main() routine which will set yydebug if it exists. For illustration purposes, the return value of yyparse() is shown.

    yacc will produce the following *y.output* file for this parser:

```
        state 0
                $accept : _expression $end

                IDENTIFIER  shift 2
                .  error

                expression  goto 1


        state 1
                $accept :  expression_$end
                expression :  expression_- expression

                $end  accept
                -  shift 3
                .  error



        state 2
                expression :  IDENTIFIER_       (2)

                .  reduce 2



        state 3
                expression :  expression -_expression

                IDENTIFIER  shift 2
                .  error

                expression  goto 4

        state 4
                expression :  expression_- expression
                expression :  expression - expression_     (1)

                    reduce 1
```

The statistical information has been omitted.

    Assume that the inputs to *lex* and *yacc* are in the files *exp.l* and *exp.y*. We construct the parser and execute it with a correct input:

```
yacc -dv exp.y
lex exp.l
cc -DYYDEBUG y.tab.c lex.yy.c -ll -o exp
exp
a - b - c
^D
```

In conjunction with *y.output* the tracing information[2] shows exactly how the input is processed:

```
[yydebug] push state 0
[yydebug] reading IDENTIFIER
[yydebug] push state 2
[yydebug] reduce by (2), uncover 0
[yydebug] push state 1
[yydebug] reading '-'
[yydebug] push state 3
[yydebug] reading IDENTIFIER
[yydebug] push state 2
[yydebug] reduce by (2), uncover 3
[yydebug] push state 4
[yydebug] reduce by (1), uncover 0
[yydebug] push state 1
[yydebug] reading '-'
[yydebug] push state 3
[yydebug] reading IDENTIFIER
[yydebug] push state 2
[yydebug] reduce by (2), uncover 3
[yydebug] push state 4
[yydebug] reduce by (1), uncover 0
[yydebug] push state 1
[yydebug] reading [end of file]
yyparse() == 0
```

It is easy to see that in state 4 formulation (1)

```
expression : expression '-' expression
```

is reduced *before* the second − is read. The recognition is successful, and yyparse() returns a function value of zero.

In contrast, consider the same grammar with the disambiguating rule defining − to be *right*-associative:

```
%token  IDENTIFIER
%right  '-'
%%
expression
        : expression '-' expression
        | IDENTIFIER
```

---

[2] Sections 8 and 9 in the appendix discuss slight modifications to */usr/lib/yaccpar* which we have made to improve error messages generated by the parser and to produce better tracing output. The modified version is used throughout the book. The standard version will display the numerical values of the terminal symbols, and there are instances where the information is destroyed *before* it is displayed!

The transition matrix remains the same, except for state 4:

```
state 4
        expression :  expression_- expression
        expression :  expression - expression      (1)

            shift 3
            reduce 1
```

Now − associates to the right, the rightmost − phrase must be reduced first, and consequently *all* − operators must be pushed onto the *yacc* stack. The algorithm employed by yyparse() requires less space on the stack for left-recursive rules and left-associative operators.

The same input produces the following trace:

```
[yydebug] push state 0
[yydebug] reading IDENTIFIER
[yydebug] push state 2
[yydebug] reduce by (2), uncover 0
[yydebug] push state 1
[yydebug] reading '-'
[yydebug] push state 3
[yydebug] reading IDENTIFIER
[yydebug] push state 2
[yydebug] reduce by (2), uncover 3
[yydebug] push state 4
[yydebug] reading '-'
[yydebug] push state 3
[yydebug] reading IDENTIFIER
[yydebug] push state 2
[yydebug] reduce by (2), uncover 3
[yydebug] push state 4
[yydebug] reading [end of file]
[yydebug] reduce by (1), uncover 3
[yydebug] push state 4
[yydebug] reduce by (1), uncover 0
[yydebug] push state 1
yyparse() == 0
```

It is easy to see that now the interesting reductions with formulation (1) both take place *after* the end of file has been encountered.

The trace is perhaps more instructive if we use the erroneous input

```
a - -
```

In the left-associative case, the output is

```
[yydebug] push state 0
[yydebug] reading IDENTIFIER
[yydebug] push state 2
[yydebug] reduce by (2), uncover 0
[yydebug] push state 1
[yydebug] reading '-'
[yydebug] push state 3
[yydebug] reading '-'
[error 1] line 1 near "-": expecting: IDENTIFIER
```

```
[yydebug] recovery pops 3, uncovers 1
[yydebug] recovery pops 1, uncovers 0
[yydebug] recovery pops 0, stack is empty
yyparse() == 1
```

Consulting *y.output*, we can see that in state 3 only an IDENTIFIER will be accepted by the parser — which is what our improved error message indicates, too. The trace shows how we got into state 3, and it also shows that yyparse() eliminates its entire stack once the input error has been encountered; in this case the value one is returned. We will deal more with error recovery in chapter 4.

Finally, consider the following modification to the grammar:

```
%token   IDENTIFIER
%nonassoc '-'
%%

expression
        : expression '-' expression
        | IDENTIFIER
```

Now − has been marked as non-associative, i.e., a sequence of subtractions is not legal. *y.output* shows the corresponding change for state 4 in the transition matrix:

```
state 4
        expression :  expression_- expression
        expression :  expression - expression_      (1)

        -   error
        .   reduce 1
```

Tracing the input

```
a - b - c
```

shows where this version of the grammar is illogical:

```
[yydebug] push state 0
[yydebug] reading IDENTIFIER
[yydebug] push state 2
[yydebug] reduce by (2), uncover 0
[yydebug] push state 1
[yydebug] reading '-'
[yydebug] push state 3
[yydebug] reading IDENTIFIER
[yydebug] push state 2
[yydebug] reduce by (2), uncover 3
[yydebug] push state 4
[yydebug] reading '-'
[error 1] line 1 near "-": syntax error
[yydebug] recovery pops 4, uncovers 3
[yydebug] recovery pops 3, uncovers 1
[yydebug] recovery pops 1, uncovers 0
[yydebug] recovery pops 0, stack is empty
yyparse() == 1
```

With a we shift to state 2 and reduce this IDENTIFIER as an expression; back in state 0 we accept the expression and goto state 1. − b is acceptable, we shift from state 1 to state 3 and state 2, where the IDENTIFIER b is once again reduced as an expression. This time, however, we rediscover state 3 on the stack and with expression we goto state 4. Here − selects the error operation in the transition matrix!

If we were looking for a flaw in the grammar, we would now wonder *why* − is unacceptable in state 4. Comparing states 1 and 4, we can see that the configuration

```
expression : expression_- expression
```

results in two different transition matrix entries for −. This is only possible if a strange disambiguating rule was specified: we have found our artificial error.

While the example may look obscure, the debugging technique is not: practical experience shows that it is usually quite easy to locate misunderstood spots in a grammar by following the yydebug trace through *y.output*. Untangling the effects of strange disambiguating rules, as we did in the last example, is perhaps the most difficult tracing and debugging job.

3.5 User-defined terminal symbols

Identifier and Constant are really classes of terminal symbols. While the parser is only interested in the class as such for sentence recognition, we will later need the actual value of the terminal symbol for further processing. Let us construct a simple desk calculator without variables:

```
/*
 *      desk calculator
 */

%token  Constant
%left   '+' '-'
%left   '*' '/'
%%

line
        : /* empty */
        | line expression '\n'
                { printf("%d\n", $2); }

expression
        : expression '+' expression
                { $$ = $1 + $3; }
        | expression '-' expression
                { $$ = $1 - $3; }
        | expression '*' expression
                { $$ = $1 * $3; }
        | expression '/' expression
                { $$ = $1 / $3; }
        | '(' expression ')'
                { $$ = $2; }
        | Constant
                /* $$ = $1; */
```

The text enclosed by braces can be viewed as a comment expressing how a formulation is to be interpreted:

```
expression : expression '+' expression
{   $$      =     $1     +     $3;  }
```

"If we have found two instances of expression connected by a + operator, we need to add their actual values; the result is the actual value of the reduced expression."

```
expression : '(' expression ')'
{   $$      =         $2;       }
```

"If we have found an instance of expression enclosed in parentheses, the actual value of the reduced expression is that of the *second* symbol in the formulation."

```
expression : Constant
/*  $$      =   $1; */
```

"If we have found a Constant, the actual value of the reduced expression is that of the *first* symbol in the formulation, i.e., it is the actual value of the Constant."

```
line : line expression '\n'
{ printf("%d\n", $2      );}
```

"If we have found a complete line, we should print the actual value of the *second* symbol in the formulation."

In fact, the braces do not contain mere comments. *yacc* permits us to specify after each formulation an *action*, C statements enclosed in braces. The action will be executed if and when the formulation is reduced.

yyparse() maintains a value stack in parallel to the state stack introduced in section 3.1. Whenever a symbol is accepted, i.e., once the current state is pushed onto the state stack during a shift or goto operation, an associated value is pushed onto the value stack.

The value to be pushed during a shift operation, i.e., during acceptance of a terminal symbol, is taken from the global int variable yylval defined by *yacc*; it can be set by the lexical analyzer for the terminal symbol. In the present example, we must place the actual value of a Constant there:

```
%{
/*
 *      lexical analyzer for desk calculator
 */

#include "y.tab.h"
extern int yylval;
%}
%%

[0-9]+              { yylval = atoi(yytext); return Constant; }
[ \t]+              ;
\n                  |
                    return yytext[0];
```

The library function `atoi()` computes the integer value of a string of digits. This value is recorded in `yylval` as the actual value of the `Constant`.

The value to be pushed during a goto operation, i.e., during acceptance of a non-terminal symbol produced by a reduce operation, is taken from the global variable `yyval` defined by *yacc*; it can be set from within the action executed during the reduce operation.

As the example shows, the action usually needs to access the values placed on the value stack during acceptance of the symbols for the formulation which is about to be reduced. The notation `$i` within an action represents the value for the *i*th symbol in the formulation presently on the value stack; the notation `$$` represents `yyval`, i.e., it represents the value which will be pushed onto the value stack during acceptance of the non-terminal symbol by the goto operation following the reduction.

The action

```
{ $$ = $1; }
```

is supplied by default. It states that the value stack entry of the first symbol in the formulation will become the value stack entry of the non-terminal symbol to which the formulation is reduced.

Our desk calculator works as advertised. For each `Constant`, the lexical analyzer provides the actual value in `yylval` which `yyparse()` places on the value stack. Once a formulation such as

```
expression : expression '-' expression
```

is reduced, the associated action

```
{ $$ = $1 - $3; }
```

computes the appropriate difference, which is pushed onto the value stack following the reduction. The `printf()` function call at the top shows the value of each expression line presented to the desk calculator.

3.6 Typing the value stack

`yylval`, `yyval`, and the value stack can be used to hold a large variety of information. By default the value stack consists of `int` elements. For our desk calculator `double` elements may actually be more interesting. In a compiler, `yylval` will most likely hold a pointer to a symbol table entry for each "large" terminal symbol. Unfortunately, `double` values — and on certain machines even pointers — cannot be stored and retrieved from `int` variables.

The value stack maintained by the parser can be typed from within a *yacc* specification. In this section we will describe a way of typing the value stack which is entirely transparent to *yacc* itself; a more elaborate typing facility which prompts *yacc* to perform rather extensive semantic checks will be discussed in section 5.4.

`yylval`, `yyval`, and the value stack are defined in the parser to be of the type YYS-TYPE. YYSTYPE itself is defined *with the C preprocesor* as `int`, unless an explicit definition is supplied in the first part of the *yacc* specification. Transparent to *yacc*, this definition can be supplied as follows:

```
%{
#define YYSTYPE double
%}

%%

/* grammar, etc. */
```

Just as in a *lex* specification, text in the first part of a *yacc* specification enclosed in %{ and %} is copied into the generated parser. The text is placed near the beginning of the output file so that default definitions made by *yacc* can be overwritten.

If we define the value stack to be double, we of course need to modify the lexical analyzer for the desk calculator a bit. yylval now is double, too, and we must convert digit strings appropriately:

```
%{
/*
 *        lexical analyzer for `double' desk calculator
 */

#include "y.tab.h"
extern double yylval, atof();
%}

digits          ([0-9]+)
pt              "."
sign            [+-]?
exponent        ([eE]{sign}{digits})

%%

{digits}({pt}{digits}?)?{exponent}?      |
{digits}?{pt}{digits}{exponent}?              { yylval = atof(yytext);
                                                return Constant;
                                              }

[ \t]+                  ;
\n                      |
                        return yytext[0];
```

The example shows how a rather general class of floating point constants involving digits, a decimal point, more digits, and an optional exponent which may be optionally signed, can be recognized using *lex* and converted using the library function atof().

This technique of typing the value stack is quite convenient to use and it does not require any changes to the grammar itself. It has a subtle problem, however. YYSTYPE is a defined name. The desired type for the value stack must be represented as a *type name*, i.e., as a single identifier or as a structure specification. The replacement text for YYSTYPE can in particular *not* be a pointer type specification! Such a specification must instead be associated with an identifier through a typedef construct and the identifier can then be used as a replacement text for YYSTYPE:

CHAPTER 3 LANGUAGE RECOGNITION 55

```
typedef char *  CHAR_PTR;
#define YYSTYPE CHAR_PTR
```

Here the identifier used as a type name is CHAR_PTR. The technique is not exactly pretty, but it is required since the definition

```
#define YYSTYPE char *
```

would *not* be factored correctly within *yaccpar*.

3.7 Example

It is time for a *sampleC* formatter with indentation. It turns out that our current grammar needs to be slightly modified: we need to associate an action with each terminal symbol, which will cause that terminal symbol to be printed. This could, of course, be done by the lexical analyzer alone, but we would then not be able to indent certain statements properly depending on syntax and context. A mixture of outputs generated by the lexical analyzer and by actions in the grammar will fail miserably: the parser is allowed to call the lexical analyzer for one terminal symbol look-ahead, and it will do so "sometimes".

To understand what we are trying to construct, consider the following *sampleC* program, which does nothing, syntactically correct, typographically badly arranged:

```
/*
 *      formatting demonstration
 */
main(a,b) int a,b; {
a=b;
{a;b;}
if (a==b) {a;b;}
if (a==b+1) a; else b;
while (a==b) {a; break; continue;}
return;
;
}
int f() {int x;int y; return nothing; }
```

Indentation is certainly a matter of individual taste. We expect to obtain the following output from our formatter:

```
main(a, b)
        int     a, b;
{
        a = b;
        {
                a;
                b;
        }
        if (a == b)
        {
                a;
                b;
        }
        if (a == b + 1)
```

```
                    a;
        else
                    b;
        while (a == b)
        {
                    a;
                    break;
                    continue;
        }
        return;
        ;
    }

    int     f()
    {       int     x;
            int     y;

            return nothing;
    }
```

Some terminal symbols, most notably braces and else, need special treatment: they control indentation. This is a very good example of the occasional need to pass context-related information between actions in a grammar: else causes indentation, but our indentation style is such that an immediately following compound statement should have its leading and trailing braces still at the current indentation level, to save on total width. Hence we pass some information through static variables.

The formatting actions are specified using certain mnemonics. They are defined in a separate file *fmt.h*, which also contains typing information for the *yacc* value stack:

```
/*
 *      formatting call mnemonic parameters
 */

#define IN      1               /* margin inward */
#define EX      (-1)            /* margin outward */
#define AT      0               /* margin as is */

/*
 *      yacc value stack type (pass texts!)
 */

typedef char * CHAR_PTR;
#define YYSTYPE CHAR_PTR
```

The formatter uses certain basic routines which are responsible for all output generation. The out() routine could additionally monitor the width of the generated output, and could insert additional line and page breaks as needed. The basic routines are kept in *fmt.c*:

```
/*
 *      sample c -- utilities for formatter
 */

#include <stdio.h>
```

```
#include "fmt.h"

/*
 *      rudimentary symbol table routine:
 *              save text of every symbol.
 */

s_lookup(yylex)
        int yylex;              /* Constant or Identifier */
{       extern YYSTYPE yylval;  /* semantic value for parser */
        extern char yytext[];   /* text value of symbol */
        extern char * strsave();

        yylval = strsave(yytext);
}

/*
 *      formatter calls:
 *
 *      at(AT)          no-op
 *      at(IN)          set margin inward
 *      at(EX)          set margin outward
 *      nl(delta)       emit newline, at(delta)
 *      cond(IN)        nl(IN)
 *      cond(EX)        if directly preceded by cond(IN): at(EX)
 *      uncond(AT)      nl(AT)
 *      uncond(EX)      unless just after uncond(AT): at(EX)
 *      out(s)          emit string s
 *
 *      Margin settings take effect just prior to first out(s) on
 *      the new line. 'cond' calls fiddle with braces and else.
 */

static int lmargin = 0;  /* left margin, in tabs */
static int atmargin = 1; /* set: we are at left margin */
static int condflag = 0; /* managed by cond(), = 0 by out() */
static int uncdflag = 0; /* managed by uncond(),  = 0 by out() */

at(delta)
        int delta;
{
        lmargin += delta;
}

cond(delta)
        int delta;
{
        switch (delta) {
        case IN:
                ++condflag;
                nl(IN);
                break;
        case EX:
                if (condflag)
                {       at(EX);
                        condflag = 0;
```

```
                        }
                }
        }

        uncond(delta)
                int delta;
        {
                switch (delta) {
                case AT:
                        ++uncdflag;
                        nl(AT);
                        break;
                case EX:
                        if (! uncdflag)
                                at(EX);
                }
        }

        nl(delta)
                int delta;
        {
                at(delta);
                putchar('\n');
                atmargin = 1;
        }

        out(s)
                char *s;
        {
                if (atmargin)
                {       register int i;

                        for (i = 0; i < lmargin; i++)
                                putchar('\t');
                        atmargin = 0;
                }
                fputs(s, stdout);
                condflag = uncdflag = 0;
        }
```

strsave() is a handy function mentioned in [Ker78b] which dynamically saves the string passed as an argument. See section 3 in the appendix. This is sufficient as a symbol table for the present problem.

Except for the addition of explicit rules for each terminal symbol together with actions to arrange for the printing of each terminal symbol, the input to *yacc* remains almost unchanged; we therefore show mostly those parts which needed to be changed or extended:

```
        /*
         *      sample c
         *      syntax analysis
         *      formatting actions
         *      (s/r conflict: one on ELSE)
         */
```

```
%{
#include "fmt.h"            /* formatter action mnemonics */
%}

/*
 *      terminal symbols
 */

/*
 *      precedence table
 */

%%

program

definitions

definition
        : function_definition
        | int function_definition
        | declaration

function_definition
        : identifier lp optional_parameter_list rp
                { nl(IN); }
          parameter_declarations
                { at(EX); }
          compound_statement
                { nl(AT); }

optional_parameter_list

parameter_list
        : identifier
        | parameter_list co identifier

parameter_declarations

parameter_declaration
        : int parameter_declarator_list sc

parameter_declarator_list
        : identifier
        | parameter_declarator_list co identifier

compound_statement
        : lr declarations
                { nl(AT); }
          statements rr

declarations

declaration
        : int declarator_list sc
```

```
declarator_list
        : identifier
        | declarator_list co identifier

statements

statement
        : expression sc
        | sc
        | break sc
        | continue sc
        | return sc
        | return
                { out(" "); }
          expression sc
        | compound_statement
        | if_prefix statement
                { uncond(EX); }
        | if_prefix statement else statement
                { uncond(EX); }
        | loop_prefix statement
                { uncond(EX); }

if_prefix
        : if lp expression rp
                { cond(IN); }

loop_prefix
        : while lp expression rp
                { cond(IN); }

expression
        : binary
        | expression co binary

binary
        : identifier
        | constant
        | lp expression rp
        | identifier lp optional_argument_list rp
        | pp identifier              %prec PP
        | mm identifier              %prec PP
        | binary pl binary           %prec '+'
        | binary mi binary           %prec '+'
        | binary mu binary           %prec '*'
        | binary di binary           %prec '*'
        | binary rm binary           %prec '*'
        | binary gt binary           %prec '>'
        | binary lt binary           %prec '>'
        | binary ge binary           %prec '>'
        | binary le binary           %prec '>'
        | binary eq binary           %prec EQ
        | binary ne binary           %prec EQ
        | binary an binary           %prec '&'
        | binary xo binary           %prec '^'
        | binary or binary           %prec '|'
```

```
                  | identifier as binary          %prec '='
                  | identifier pe binary          %prec '='
                  | identifier me binary          %prec '='
                  | identifier te binary          %prec '='
                  | identifier de binary          %prec '='
                  | identifier re binary          %prec '='

       optional_argument_list

       argument_list
             : binary
             | argument_list co binary

       /*
        *       printing the terminal symbols
        */

       int     : INT          { out("int\t"); }
       identifier : Identifier { out($1); }
       lp        : '('         { out("("); }
       rp        : ')'         { out(")"); }
       co        : ','         { out(", "); }
       sc        : ';'         { out(";"); nl(AT); }
       break     : BREAK       { out("break"); }
       continue: CONTINUE      { out("continue"); }
       return  : RETURN        { out("return"); }
       lr        : '{'         { cond(EX); out("{\t"); at(IN); }
       rr        : '}'         { at(EX); out("}"); uncond(AT); }
       if        : IF          { out("if "); }
       else      : ELSE        { at(EX); out("else"); cond(IN); }
       while     : WHILE       { out("while "); }
       constant: Constant      { out($1); }
       pp        : PP          { out(" ++ "); }
       mm        : MM          { out(" -- "); }
       pl        : '+'         { out(" + "); }
       mi        : '-'         { out(" - "); }
       mu        : '*'         { out(" * "); }
       di        : '/'         { out(" / "); }
       rm        : '%'         { out(" % "); }
       gt        : '>'         { out(" > "); }
       lt        : '<'         { out(" < "); }
       ge        : GE          { out(" >= "); }
       le        : LE          { out(" <= "); }
       eq        : EQ          { out(" == "); }
       ne        : NE          { out(" != "); }
       an        : '&'         { out(" & "); }
       xo        : '^'         { out(" ^ "); }
       or        : '|'         { out(" | "); }
       as        : '='         { out(" = "); }
       pe        : PE          { out(" += "); }
       me        : ME          { out(" -= "); }
       te        : TE          { out(" *= "); }
       de        : DE          { out(" /= "); }
       re        : RE          { out(" %= "); }
```

%prec is a *yacc* operator which may follow a formulation. This is a disambiguating technique similar to mentioning operators in %left, %right, and %nonassoc precedence statements. %prec must be followed by a terminal symbol to indicate the precedence. This construct is often used in the context of unary operators; here it is necessary because we have replaced all terminal operator symbols by non-terminal symbols so that we might group the output actions together.

In order to illustrate the basic technique used in designing the cooperation of the formatting actions, let us compare the sequence of events in formatting

```
if (1)
            1;
```

and

```
if (1)
{
            1;
}
```

In both cases, cond(IN); is called during the reduction of if_prefix and it sets the left margin inward. In the first case, statement turns out to be an expression and the indentation remains. In the second case, statement will be a compound_statement and therefore lr will be reduced for the left brace before any other reduction takes place. The action during reduction of lr calls cond(EX); which notes from condflag that a call cond(IN); has just taken place. The left brace can therefore be exdented and placed underneath if. As promised, static variables are used to pass context information between neighboring reductions. The technique has little to recommend it other than that it avoids a lot of devious rewriting of the grammar itself.

The formulation of compound_statement shows a second method of specifying actions:

```
compound_statement
        : lr declarations
                { nl(AT); }
        statements rr
```

Our formatting style requires that an empty line follow declarations. The call nl(AT); will issue the blank line. An action can be placed anywhere in a formulation; if it does not follow the entire formulation, *yacc* will generate an anonymous non-terminal symbol in place of the action and define the non-terminal symbol with a empty formulation followed by the action. The formulation shown above is really expanded as follows:

```
compound_statement
        : lr declarations $$123 statements rr

$$123
        : /* empty */
                { nl(AT); }
```

Actions cannot be placed entirely at will in this fashion; the anonymous non-terminal symbols can introduce conflicts.

One problem has not been discussed: this formatter only deals with a source file that has been preprocessed, i.e., which contains no comments! In a realistic implementation, the lexical analyzer would have to collect the comments, and pass them to the formatting routine, probably attached to terminal symbols. This involves a significant amount of bookkeeping, and the problem of formatting comments is nontrivial.

3.8 Problems

1. Extend the desk calculator example so that it uses variables. A very simple extension is to predefine twenty-six variables, a through z, and the storage in which to save their values. A more interesting problem is to allow arbitrary variable names; in this case, storage both for the strings that name the variables and for their values should be acquired dynamically.

2. The formatting style used in section 3.7 may not be your favorite format. Modify the formatting program given in that section so that it conforms to your preferred standards.

3. Write a formatting program for a subset of Pascal, perhaps the one used for problem 1 of section 1.8.

4. The formatter given in section 3.7 produces a blank line following each function. This means that if the last definition in a file is a function_definition, there will be a useless blank line as the last line of the output. Change the program to suppress this extra blank line. Hint: it may be easier to control the blank line if you emit it before each function, rather than after.

5. Write a formatting program for EBNF. It should display an EBNF grammar in a standard format, such as the one suggested in section 1.7. It is convenient to start with the solution to problem 3 of section 1.8.

6. Write a program which will convert a grammar written in EBNF to BNF. Hint: for reasons of efficiency internal to *yacc*, use left-recursion for iterations. See the discussion of the treatment of its stack by *yacc* in the left- and right-recursive definitions of

```
        expression : expression '-' expression
```

in section 3.4.

7. Modify the standard */usr/lib/yaccpar* to produce the trace format shown in this chapter. For some important hints, see section A.8 in the appendix.

8. In the last paragraph of the previous section, it was mentioned that inclusion of comments in the formatted output is somewhat difficult. An approach to the solution of this problem was also suggested. Modify the example from that section, or the program from question 2, 3, or 4 above, to display comments. Suggestion: if a comment is the first "thing" on a line, display it at the beginning of the line (perhaps at the current indenting level). If the comment follows something else on the same line, display it at a user-settable or predetermined "tab" position.

9. Using techniques similar to those used in solving the previous problem, write a program which will display preprocessor lines (lines with # in column 1) as part of a program.

Real compilers deal mostly with incorrect input files. This chapter discusses how we can make our parser robust against input errors. We first use tracing to show what happens inside the parser when an input error is encountered. It turns out that thus far the parser would "fall off the stack" during an error operation. However, *yacc* provides a special error terminal symbol to influence the parsing algorithm. In section 4.2 we demonstrate what happens if a parser is properly prepared to cope with an error.

The problem in general is to build robust grammars using error symbols in formulations added to some rules. Fortunately we found a straightforward way to extend a number of constructs frequently found in programming languages in such a way that they cope with *any* error. Our technique is presented in section 4.3, and in section 4.5 we show how a robust recognizer for *sampleC* is defined, and how we can fully demonstrate its behavior in case of erroneous inputs.

4.1 The problem

Thus far, our parser can recognize and perhaps manipulate a sentence, i.e., a *correct* input file. One of the examples in section 3.4 showed what happens if we present the incorrect input

```
a - -
```

to a parser based on the rule

```
expression
        : expression '-' expression
        | IDENTIFIER
```

with − defined to be left-associative. yyparse() falls off the stack:

```
[yydebug] push state 0
[yydebug] reading IDENTIFIER
[yydebug] push state 2
[yydebug] reduce by (2), uncover 0
[yydebug] push state 1
[yydebug] reading '-'
[yydebug] push state 3
[yydebug] reading '-'
[error 1] line 1 near "-": expecting: IDENTIFIER
[yydebug] recovery pops 3, uncovers 1
[yydebug] recovery pops 1, uncovers 0
[yydebug] recovery pops 0, stack is empty
yyparse() == 1
```

The second − in state 3 leads to an error operation in the transition matrix:

```
state 3
        expression :  expression -_expression

        IDENTIFIER  shift 2
```

```
error

expression  goto 4
```

Once the error message has been issued, yyparse() seems to remove all states from the stack — obviously looking for something. Since the stack is cleared in the process, yyparse() returns with a function value of one, and the recognition procedure is aborted on encountering the first error in the input!

4.2 Basic techniques

Our lexical analyzers usually have the following entry at the end of the pattern table:

```
return yytext[0];
```

The pattern is intended to pick up all single character operators. However, this entry will return the integer value of *any* single character as function value of yylex(), i.e., as a terminal symbol, as long as the character has not been recognized by an earlier pattern.

Unexpected input characters are thus passed from the lexical analyzer to the parser as if they were legitimate terminal symbols, represented by single characters. This results in a uniform treatment of all input errors. An alternative approach at this level would be to have the lexical analyzer report its own problems, and then to ignore illegal characters; however, in this case it is hard to avoid cascades of messages.

At the symbol level, we can add formulations to the grammar that are probable although illegal. This technique makes our recognizer more tolerant than the language designer intended it to be. While we can forgive the most frequent user errors in this fashion, the technique does not have a high probability of complete success — it is nearly impossible to exactly predict an incorrect input sequence.

A better approach is to treat an input error as a special case of a terminal symbol: error is a predefined terminal symbol for *yacc*. error can be used in formulations just like a terminal symbol; however, error is (normally) not produced by a call to the lexical analyzer. Instead, the parser believes error to be the next terminal symbol if the actual next terminal symbol leads to an error operation in the transition matrix for the current state. Once the error symbol has been internally generated in this fashion, and the obligatory error message issued, yyparse() will set out to accept error almost like any other symbol.

Consider the following modification to the rule above:

```
expression
        : expression '-' expression
        | IDENTIFIER
        | error
```

A parser based on this grammar will silently accept erroneous input. To understand why this is the case, we need to once again follow the traces of a few examples. *yacc* will produce the following *y.output* file:

```
state 0
        $accept : _expression $end
```

```
        error  shift 3
        IDENTIFIER  shift 2
        .  error

        expression  goto 1

state 1
        $accept :  expression_$end
        expression :  expression_- expression

        $end  accept
        -  shift 4
        .  error


state 2
        expression :  IDENTIFIER_     (2)

        .  reduce 2


state 3
        expression :  error_     (3)

        .  reduce 3


state 4
        expression :  expression -_expression

        error  shift 3
        IDENTIFIER  shift 2
        .  error

        expression  goto 5

state 5
        expression :  expression_- expression
        expression :  expression - expression_     (1)

        .  reduce 1
```

Note that error appears as an operation in a number of states; in state 0 and in state 4 it also appears as a terminal symbol, for which the operation shift 3 is present in the transition matrix.

Let us now see how this parser reacts to the erroneous input

        a - - b

The trace shows that up to reading the second − the parser acts just like before:

```
        [yydebug] push state 0
        [yydebug] reading IDENTIFIER
        [yydebug] push state 2
        [yydebug] reduce by (2), uncover 0
        [yydebug] push state 1
```

```
[yydebug] reading '-'
[yydebug] push state 4
[yydebug] reading '-'
[error 1] line 1 near "-": expecting: IDENTIFIER
```

We are in state 4, and the new − has lead to the error operation. As just discussed, yyparse() will now assume that the next terminal symbol is error. The transition matrix prescribes that the symbol error is to be accepted, and we can move on to state 3:

```
[yydebug] accepting $error
[yydebug] push state 3
```

We can follow the process using the transition matrix as shown in *y.output*: In state 3, a reduction is possible, an expression is manufactured from the error, and with it we reach state 5 from state 4 revealed on the stack.

```
[yydebug] reduce by (3), uncover 4
[yydebug] push state 5
[yydebug] reduce by (1), uncover 0
[yydebug] push state 1
[yydebug] push state 4
```

Now another reduction is possible, we reach state 0 on the stack, a goto operation for the reduced expression takes us to state 1, and there we are able to finally accept the − symbol from the input! Things are back to normal, and recognition can be completed successfully:

```
[yydebug] reading IDENTIFIER
[yydebug] push state 2
[yydebug] reduce by (2), uncover 4
[yydebug] push state 5
[yydebug] reduce by (1), uncover 0
[yydebug] push state 1
[yydebug] reading [end of file]
yyparse() = 0
```

Error recovery, in fact, consisted of *inserting* the error symbol between the two − symbols in the input. The resulting input was acceptable to the extended grammar. This, however, is not the whole story — sometimes the error recovery mechanism must *discard* an input symbol to keep going. This is why error is treated by *yacc* and yyparse() quite differently from normal terminal symbols. Let us see what happens if

```
a + - b
```

is to be recognized. Here, + is an illegal character, passed by yylex() just like a valid terminal symbol, and it will certainly have to be discarded:

```
[yydebug] push state 0
[yydebug] reading IDENTIFIER
[yydebug] push state 2
[yydebug] reduce by (2), uncover 0
[yydebug] push state 1
[yydebug] reading '+'
[error 1] line 1 near "+": expecting: '-'
```

This time we are in trouble in state 1. Once again the error symbol is generated internally, but unlike in state 4, in state 1 the transition matrix contains the error operation for the error symbol! (In *y.output,* . denotes "all other symbols".)

At this point, yyparse() starts popping its stack. The function is looking for a state *on the stack* in which the error symbol can be accepted. If no such state is on the stack, i.e., if we have not previously encountered a configuration for which error was the next symbol, yyparse() will clear the entire stack and then terminate with a function value of one.

In the example we are "lucky". We find state 0 on the stack, and in this state error is acceptable. Once again we shift to state 3, manufacture an expression, return to state 0 on the stack and goto state 1 with the expression:

```
[yydebug] recovery pops 1, uncovers 0
[yydebug] accepting $error
[yydebug] push state 3
[yydebug] reduce by (3), uncover 0
[yydebug] push state 1
```

It looks like nothing has happened: we are once more in state 1, and + is still the next terminal symbol! Now, however, yyparse() remembers that no shift operation has taken place since the last error. In order to avoid a loop, yyparse() now discards the next terminal symbol, and in this case can complete the recognition:

```
[yydebug] recovery discards '+'
[yydebug] reading '-'
[yydebug] push state 4
[yydebug] reading IDENTIFIER
[yydebug] push state 2
[yydebug] reduce by (2), uncover 4
[yydebug] push state 5
[yydebug] reduce by (1), uncover 0
[yydebug] push state 1
[yydebug] reading [end of file]
yyparse() = 0
```

Let us put the two errors together. Without a trace, the input

```
a - - b + - c
```

produces only one error message:

```
[error 1] line 1 near "-": expecting: IDENTIFIER
yyparse() = 0
```

The trace reveals that both errors are, in fact, discovered:

```
[yydebug] push state 0
[yydebug] reading IDENTIFIER
          . . .
[yydebug] reading '-'
[error 1] line 1 near "-": expecting: IDENTIFIER
[yydebug] accepting $error
          . . .
[yydebug] reading '+'
[yydebug] recovery pops 1, uncovers 0
```

```
[yydebug] accepting $error
        ...
[yydebug] recovery discards '+'
        ...
yyparse() = 0
```

In order to avoid a cascade of error messages, the parser must shift three terminal symbols beyond the point of error, before another error results in an error message. This way a cluster of errors may result in only a single error message. In this example, this explains the absence of the second error message.

With the yyerrok; action, the parser can be persuaded to feel that it has accepted enough terminal symbols, and thus to report errors in close proximity to one another.

There is a drawback, though: if yyerrok; is attached as an action to a formulation consisting only of error, yyparse() immediately believes that enough terminal symbols have been shifted, and thus can never discard an erroneous input symbol!

A more sensible example for the yyerrok; action is the following extension to our grammar:

```
expression
        : expression '-' expression
        | IDENTIFIER
                { yyerrok; }
        | error
```

Once we have seen an IDENTIFIER following an error, it is reasonable to assume we are back on the right track, and thus to request to be informed of subsequent errors. This extension will produce two error messages for our example:

```
[error 1] line 1 near "-": expecting: IDENTIFIER
[error 2] line 1 near "+": expecting: '-'
yyparse() = 0
```

The error symbol and the yyerrok; action are the *yacc* features to use in making a parser robust. The tricky problem is to employ these basic tools judiciously.

4.3 Adding the "error" symbols

The placement of error symbols is guided by the following, conflicting goals:

● as close as possible to the start symbol of the grammar.

This way there is always a point to recover from, since there should always be a state very low on the stack in which error can be accepted. The parser then is never able to clear its stack early, i.e., to not complete by recognizing the end of file from the lexical analyzer.

● as close as possible to each terminal symbol.

This way only a small amount of input would be skipped on each error. This can be improved using yyerrok; actions.

● without introducing conflicts.

This may be quite difficult. In fact, accepting shift/reduce conflicts is reasonable as long as they serve to lengthen strings. E.g., one can continue parsing an expression past an error, rather then accepting the same error at the statement level, thus trashing the rest of the expression.

Following these goals, we recommend the following typical positions for error symbols:

- into each recursive construct, i.e., into each repetition.

- preferably not at the end of a formulation.

    This should result in a robust recovery, i.e., in a recovery from which the continuation is meaningful. Adding a trailing error and yyerrok; action may lead to cascading error messages, or even to loops if the parser cannot discard input.

- non-empty lists require two error variants, one for a problem at the beginning of the list, and one for a problem at the current end of the list.

- possibly empty lists require an error symbol in the empty branch.

    If this proves impossible, add the symbol to the places where the possibly empty list is being used.

The following table is our recommendation for the placement of error symbols in the most frequent repetitive constructs[1]:

construct	EBNF	yacc input
optional sequence	x: { y }	x: /* null */
		| x y { yyerrok; }
		| x error
sequence	x: y { y }	x: y
		| x y { yyerrok; }
		| error
		| x error
list	x: y { T y }	x: y
		| x T y { yyerrok; }
		| error
		| x error
		| x error y { yyerrok; }
		| x T error

We will demonstrate the three cases in turn. In each case, we use the lexical analyzer constructed for the desk calculator in section 3.5. Error recovery for the optional sequence can be studied using the following input for *yacc*:

---

[1] This way of extending repetitive constructs has a drawback due to a bug in *yacc* (as distributed with Bell version 7, Berkeley 4.2bsd, and various derivatives): if in a state the default action is to reduce, and if the next terminal symbol cannot be shifted but error could be (e.g., on a trailing error in a rule), *yacc*'s tables dictate that the reduction take place, even if the next terminal symbol cannot be shifted subsequently. In this case error recovery takes place "too late", and the parser can, in fact, go into a loop, mistakenly reduce rules several times, etc. The 4.1bsd distribution actually contains a correction for this bug, based on [Gra79]. Essentially, in these cases all possible inputs must be enumerated, so that the error can be detected; this results in slightly larger parser tables. The correction in 4.1bsd contains a typographical error, however. A definite correction is available from the authors (S. Johnson, personal communication, 1982).

```
%{
#include <stdio.h>
#define put(x)  printf("%d ", x)
#define err(x)  fputs("err x ", stdout)
%}
%token  Constant
%%

line
        : /* empty */
        | line optional_sequence '\n'
                { putchar('\n');
                  yyerrok;
                }

optional_sequence
        : /* empty */
        | optional_sequence Constant
                { put($2);
                  yyerrok;
                }
        | optional_sequence error
                { err(1); }

%%

main(argc)
{       extern FILE * yyerfp;

        yyerfp = stderr;           /* separate listings */
        printf("yyparse() = %d\n", yyparse());
}
```

We assign stderr to our file pointer for error messages (section 3.3), so that we obtain the error messages separately from the action output. The actions are designed to exhibit the reduction behavior of this parser. The input

```
10 20

10 +
10 + 20
```

produces the output

```
10 20

10 err 1
10 err 1 20
yyparse() = 0
```

and the error messages

```
[error 1] line 3 near "+": expecting: '\n' Constant
[error 2] line 4 near "+": expecting: '\n' Constant
```

All terminal symbols are properly reduced, in spite of the input errors.

If the sequence must contain at least one element, we need to change the parser slightly:

```
sequence
        : Constant
                { put($1); }
        | sequence Constant
                { put($2);
                  yyerrok;
                }
        | error
                { err(1); }
        | sequence error
                { err(2); }
```

The same input produces

```
10  20
err  1
10 err 2
10 err 2 20
yyparse() = 0
```

and one additional error message for the empty line:

```
[error 1] line 2: expecting: Constant
[error 2] line 3 near "+": expecting: '\n' Constant
[error 3] line 4 near "+": expecting: '\n' Constant
```

Again, all terminal symbols have been properly reduced.

The list, a sequence with at least one element, and delimiters between any two elements, has more error possibilities:

```
list
        : Constant
                { put($1); }
        | list ',' Constant
                { put($3);
                  yyerrok;
                }
        | error
                { err(1); }
        | list error
                { err(2); }
        | list error Constant
                { err(3);
                  put($3);
                  yyerrok;
                }
        | list ',' error
                { err(4); }
```

The test data reflect the additional structure:

```
10 , 20

10 +
10 20
10 ,
10 + 20
```

The output

```
10 20
err 1
10 err 2
10 err 3 20
10 err 4
10 err 2
yyparse() = 0
```

and the error messages

```
[error 1] line 2: expecting: Constant
[error 2] line 3 near "+": expecting: '\n' ','
[error 3] line 4 near "20": expecting: '\n' ','
[error 4] line 5: expecting: Constant
[error 5] line 6 near "+": expecting: '\n' ','
```

demonstrate that we are able to recover in all cases. Unfortunately, the case

```
10 + 20
```

is recovered through the rule

```
list : list error
```

and the second element of the list is discarded! If we eliminate this formulation, however, recognition does not terminate properly in the case of a trailing error.

Our recommendations for the placement of error symbols do not guarantee that a useful input symbol is not ignored in some error situations. Actual use, however, has convinced us that these recommendations lead to very robust parsers for common language constructs in a systematic fashion.

4.4 Adding the "yyerrok" actions

yyerrok; should be placed following terminal symbols at all points at which a formulation can end in error and is then followed by a reasonably significant terminal symbol. The repetitive constructs described above have already included the relevant actions.

This way, once the terminal symbol is reduced, any subsequent error would again be reported — the three-symbol-rule notwithstanding.

In effect, some symbols become rather important, in *sampleC* for example

```
sc      ;
rp      )
rr      }
```

Comma does not become important, since in repetitive constructs it may or may not be followed by error; it is thus treated there.

For these very important symbols we simply create "terminal action rules", just as we did for all terminal symbols in the formatter.

4.5 Example

We add error symbols and yyerrok; actions to the *sampleC* grammar developed in section 1.6 exactly as prescribed by the table in section 4.3. We also replace ';', ')', and '}' by non-terminal symbols as discussed in section 4.4, in order to always attach yyerrok; actions to these symbols. Once the result is submitted to *yacc*, we encounter two shift/reduce and two reduce/reduce conflicts. The file *y.output* shows the following problems:

```
40: shift/reduce conflict (shift 46, red'n 39) on error
state 40
        compound_statement :  { declarations_statements rr
        declarations :  declarations_declaration
        declarations :  declarations_error
        statements : _        (39)

        error  shift 46
        Identifier  reduce 39
                ...
        . error

        declaration  goto 45
        statements  goto 44

53: reduce/reduce conflict (red'ns 41 and 56 ) on error
53: reduce/reduce conflict (red'ns 41 and 56 ) on ;
state 53
        statements :  statements error_      (41)
        expression :  error_      (56)

        ,  reduce 56
        .  reduce 41

83: shift/reduce conflict (shift 115, red'n 49) on ELSE
state 83
        statement :  if_prefix statement_      (49)
        statement :  if_prefix statement_ELSE statement

        ELSE  shift 115
        .  reduce 49
```

The shift/reduce conflict in state 38 results from the fact that declarations and statements both are optional sequences, i.e., can be empty, consist of a single error, or have a leading or trailing error. If we accept the conflict, we will extend declarations as long as possible, which seems desirable.

The other shift/reduce conflict is the "dangling else problem" which we already had in the original grammar.

The two reduce/reduce conflicts have to do with an inability to discover the end of an expression. After replacing

```
expression
        : error
```

by

```
expression
        : error ',' binary
        | error binary
```

the reduce/reduce conflicts disappear as planned, but we have five new shift/reduce conflicts. *y.output* suggests why:

```
53: shift/reduce conflict (shift 66, red'n 41) on Identifier
53: shift/reduce conflict (shift 67, red'n 41) on Constant
53: shift/reduce conflict (shift 68, red'n 41) on (
53: shift/reduce conflict (shift 69, red'n 41) on PP
53: shift/reduce conflict (shift 70, red'n 41) on MM
state 53
        statements :    statements error_     (41)
        expression :    error_, binary
        expression :    error_binary

        Identifier  shift 66
        Constant  shift 67
        (  shift 68
        PP  shift 69
        MM  shift 70
        ,  shift 75
        .  reduce 41

        binary  goto 76
```

We need to insist on a terminal symbol prior to binary. Once we insist on the presence of a comma in all relevant formulations for expression and, for reasons of analogy also in argument_list, these shift/reduce conflicts disappear.

Finally we decide to add a few more error symbols to improve performance in certain spots:

```
if_prefix
        : IF error

loop_prefix
        : WHILE error

binary
        : '(' error rp
```

Another candidate for such a tuning modification might be the return statement.

In order to demonstrate that error recovery is successful, we add an action to each rule containing an error symbol. The changed parts of the grammar are as follows:

```
/*
 *      sample c
 *      syntax analysis with error recovery
 *      (s/r conflicts: one on ELSE, one on error)
 */

%{
#define ERROR(x) yywhere(), puts(x)
%}

/*
 *      terminal symbols
 */

/*
 *      precedence table
 */

%%

program

definitions
        : definition
        | definitions definition
                { yyerrok; }
        | error
                { ERROR("definitions: error"); }
        | definitions error
                { ERROR("definitions: definitions error"); }

definition

function_definition
        : Identifier '(' optional_parameter_list rp
          parameter_declarations compound_statement

optional_parameter_list

parameter_list
        : Identifier
        | parameter_list ',' Identifier
                { yyerrok; }
        | error
                { ERROR("parm_list: error"); }
        | parameter_list error
                { ERROR("parm_list: parm_list error"); }
        | parameter_list error Identifier
                { ERROR("parm_list: parm_list error Id");
                  yyerrok;
                }
        | parameter_list ',' error
                { ERROR("parm_list: parm_list ',' error"); }

parameter_declarations
        : /* null */
```

```
        | parameter_declarations parameter_declaration
                { yyerrok; }
        | parameter_declarations error
                { ERROR("parm_decls: parm_decls error"); }

parameter_declaration
        : INT parameter_declarator_list sc

parameter_declarator_list
        : Identifier
        | parameter_declarator_list ',' Identifier
                { yyerrok; }
        | error
                { ERROR("parm_decl_l: error"); }
        | parameter_declarator_list error
                { ERROR("parm_decl_l: parm_decl_l error"); }
        | parameter_declarator_list error Identifier
                { ERROR("parm_decl_l: parm_decl_l error Id");
                  yyerrok;
                }
        | parameter_declarator_list ',' error
                { ERROR("parm_decl_l: parm_decl_l ',' error"); }

compound_statement
        : '{' declarations statements rr

declarations
        : /* null */
        | declarations declaration
                { yyerrok; }
        | declarations error
                { ERROR("declarations: declarations error"); }

declaration
        : INT declarator_list sc

declarator_list
        : Identifier
        | declarator_list ',' Identifier
                { yyerrok; }
        | error
                { ERROR("decl_list: error"); }
        | declarator_list error
                { ERROR("decl_list: decl_list error"); }
        | declarator_list error Identifier
                { ERROR("decl_list: decl_list error Id");
                  yyerrok;
                }
        | declarator_list ',' error
                { ERROR("decl_list: decl_list ',' error"); }

statements
        : /* null */
        | statements statement
                { yyerrok; }
        | statements error
```

```
                    { ERROR("statements: statements error"); }

    statement
            : expression sc
            | sc
            | BREAK sc
            | CONTINUE sc
            | RETURN sc
            | RETURN expression sc
            | compound_statement
            | if_prefix statement
            | if_prefix statement ELSE statement
            | loop_prefix statement

    if_prefix
            : IF '(' expression rp
            | IF error
                { ERROR("if_prefix: IF error"); }

    loop_prefix
            : WHILE '(' expression rp
            | WHILE error
                { ERROR("loop_prefix: WHILE error"); }

    expression
            : binary
            | expression ',' binary
                { yyerrok; }
            | error ',' binary
                { ERROR("expression: error ',' binary");
                  yyerrok;
                }
            | expression error
                { ERROR("expression: expression error"); }
            | expression ',' error
                { ERROR("expression: expression ',' error"); }

    binary
            : Identifier
            | Constant
            | '(' expression rp
            | '(' error rp
                { ERROR("binary: '(' error ')'"); }
            | Identifier '(' optional_argument_list rp
            | PP Identifier
            | MM Identifier
            | binary '+' binary
            | binary '-' binary
            | binary '*' binary
            | binary '/' binary
            | binary '%' binary
            | binary '>' binary
            | binary '<' binary
            | binary GE binary
            | binary LE binary
            | binary EQ binary
```

```
                | binary NE binary
                | binary '&' binary
                | binary '^' binary
                | binary '|' binary
                | Identifier '=' binary
                | Identifier PE binary
                | Identifier ME binary
                | Identifier TE binary
                | Identifier DE binary
                | Identifier RE binary

        optional_argument_list

        argument_list
                : binary
                | argument_list ',' binary
                        { yyerrok; }
                | error
                        { ERROR("arg_list: error"); }
                | argument_list error
                        { ERROR("arg_list: arg_list error"); }
                | argument_list ',' error
                        { ERROR("arg_list: arg_list ',' error"); }

        /*
         *      make certain terminal symbols very important
         */

        rp      : ')'     { yyerrok; }
        sc      : ';'     { yyerrok; }
        rr      : '}'     { yyerrok; }
```

The following input file exercises the error recovery mechanisms introduced in the grammar:

```
        f1() { }
        char x;         /* 2: bad definition */
        char y;         /* this one is swallowed -- no yyerrok */

        f2() { }        /* this is parsed again */

        f3(a,
                int,    /* 7: bad parameter */
                c) { }

        f4(int          /* 10: bad parameter */
                ) { }

        f5(a, b)
                int a;
                while ; /* 15: bad declaration */
                int b;
                { }

        int a,
                while,  /* 20: bad declarator */
```

```
            b;

    f6() {
            break    /* 24: bad statement */
            break;
            return;
            }

    f7() {
            a,
            int,     /* 31: bad expression */
            b;
            }

    f8() {
            f7(a,
            int,     /* 37: bad argument */
            b);
            }
```

We obtain the following result:

```
    [error 1] line 2 near "x": expecting: '('
    line 2 near "x": definitions: definitions error
    line 2 near ";": definitions: definitions error
    line 3 near "y": definitions: definitions error
    line 3 near ";": definitions: definitions error
    [error 2] line 8 near "int": expecting: Identifier
    line 8 near "int": parm_list: parm_list ',' error
    [error 3] line 11 near "int": expecting: Identifier
    line 11 near "int": parm_list: error
    [error 4] line 16 near "while": expecting: '{' INT
    line 16 near "while": parm_decls: parm_decls error
    [error 5] line 21 near "while": expecting: Identifier
    line 21 near "while": decl_list: decl_list ',' error
    [error 6] line 26 near "break": expecting: ';'
    line 26 near "break": statements: statements error
    [error 7] line 32 near "int": expecting: '(' Ident. Const. PP MM
    line 32 near "int": expression: expression ',' error
    [error 8] line 38 near "int": expecting: '(' Ident. Const. PP MM
    line 38 near "int": arg_list: arg_list ',' error
```

The output shows that some clustered errors are not reported individually.

4.6 Problems

1. Generate an input file that can be used with the version of *sampleC* in section 4.5 to exercise every formulation involving error.

2. In the example, several errors in definitions are reported as one. How can this be improved? Try your solution with an input file containing some suitable errors.

3. Add error recovery to the desk calculator example in section 3.5, or to the one you developed for problem 1 in section 3.8. Hint: at the line level, the basic technique has been demonstrated in section 4.3. Adding error recovery to the expression level is a more challenging problem.

4. Integrate the techniques used for expression in problem 3 into the error recovery for *sampleC*.

5. Change the desk calculator of problem 3 so that after any error, it will prompt the user for a corrected input line. Hint: special care must be taken in the placement of yyerrok; statements, since it would clearly be unacceptable for the parser to discard tokens from the re-entered line as part of its response to errors in the original line.

6. Add error recovery features to the grammar produced for a Pascal subset in problem 1 of section 1.8. Test your grammar with an input file containing a suitable selection of erroneous Pascal code.

Chapter 5
Semantic Restrictions

We now turn from the general problem of robust language recognition to the more specific problem of analyzing a program text in order to produce a translated, executable version of it. The word *program* will therefore be used in place of *sentence*, i.e., it is defined as a sequence of terminal symbols, for which a unique parse tree with respect to a grammar can be built. This chapter discusses how we impose additional restrictions on a program, thus completing the *analysis* part of a compiler; the following chapters describe the synthesis of an executable version of the algorithm described by a program.

5.1 The problem

A program can be syntactically correct and still contain semantic errors. Some typical examples are the following:

In Pascal, labels are digit strings which must be declared in a label declaration before they can be used. While the lexical analyzer might return such a digit string as IntegerConstant, if it is used in a goto statement, a compiler has to verify that it is a declared label.

In Pascal, labels must be declared before they are used. In C a label is an Identifier; if it is newly introduced following goto, it is implicitly declared to be a label. In almost all languages, labels can be *defined after* they have been used. For all labels, the compiler must verify that they have, in fact, been defined.

Labels are just one — sticky — example of *scope* problems: a user-defined object is only known within a particular area of the program text, known as the *scope* of a name. In Basic, the scope of a variable name is the entire program text (with the exception of user-defined function parameter names). In Fortran, variable names are known only within a program unit, i.e., a function or subroutine; program unit names and common area names are known throughout all modules which are bound into an *image*, a file which may be executed. In Pascal and other Algol-like languages, user-defined names are known within a *block*, i.e., a syntactically delimited area of the program text which contains the definition for the name; blocks can be nested, and the definition of a name in an outer block can be hidden for the extent of an interior block by a new definition for the name in the interior block. C combines Algol block structure and the module concept of Fortran: compound statements are blocks which can be nested, can contain declarations, and limit their scope; function names are known globally and need not necessarily be declared before use. It is the compiler's responsibility to monitor the correct use of user-defined names within their respective scopes, as well as to generate code providing appropriate access to the various objects.

Names cannot in general be declared twice in the same context, e.g., two parameters may not have the same name, two local variables in the same block must use different names, two components of the same struct, union, or record construct must differ. While C permits struct and other names to be identical, some versions of C require component names to be distinct even for different structures.

Declarations in a program convey the intended use of a name to the compiler. Once the use has been agreed upon, abuse must be prevented. Consider:

In most languages — with the notable exception of PL/I, or deliberately lenient tools like *awk* — strings and numerical values cannot be combined, e.g., for addition. In Pascal, *mixed mode* expressions, i.e., combinations of real and integer values, are permitted for most operators, but certain restrictions apply: div expresses integer division only, / delivers a real result even for two integer operands, := permits assignment from integer to real but not conversely, etc.

Operators change their precise meaning based on the types of their operands. In some dialects of Basic, + denotes addition for numerical values and concatenation for strings. In Pascal, + denotes addition for numerical values and union for set values — at least in common representations of the language. In C, + can describe involved address manipulations if it combines a pointer and an integer value. Numerically, and as a machine instruction, + is quite a different operation between integer or between floating point values: the result of the integer operation is independent of the order of its operands and of implicitly placed parentheses, whereas the floating point result can critically depend on it.

Component selection in struct, union, or record constructs requires in general that the selector name belong to the structure of the variable from which the selection is to be made, i.e., operators like ., ^, and -> have rather strict requirements for the types of their operands. C is — intentionally — rather permissive in this respect.

Enumerating a fixed, maximum number of identical phrases is a cumbersome technique in BNF. It also cannot handle some features usually found in programming languages. Consider:

Basic arrays normally may have one or two dimensions. Some versions of Fortran limit arrays to seven dimensions. A compiler must limit the number of indexing expressions in general, and it must verify for each specific array reference that the correct, individual number of indices is used. In Pascal or C, arbitrarily many dimensions can be defined; however, the number of indices used determines the data type of the reference.

A similar problem arises with function parameters. Number and types of the arguments are predefined for built-in functions, and follow from the definition for user-defined functions. A Pascal compiler must at least verify that argument values and parameters fit together; C is quite permissive in this respect. A PL/I compiler is even responsible for argument conversion.

Parameter passing poses another problem: if, as in Pascal, a subprogram may indicate a desire to modify some of its arguments, care must be taken to insure that only suitable arguments are handed down. In Fortran, all parameters can be modified, but only certain arguments (*l-values* in the sense of C) will be changed as a consequence — this is a code generation problem.

Most semantic restrictions deal with user-defined objects, i.e., constants, types, variables, subprograms and labels. We will need a symbol table, into which all information from declarations and definitions is entered, and which is consulted whenever a user-defined name is referenced.

Some semantic restrictions, however, deal with problems which defy a simple syntactic resolution. Consider:

In Pascal or C, all constants in the context of case must be distinct. In C, case and default labels must be positioned within a statement dependent on a switch clause; interestingly enough, this dependent statement need not even be a compound statement!

Similarly, the break and continue statements of C must be placed in a context from which the desired escape makes sense.

Restrictions like these require a certain amount of local testing associated with particular constructs. Our implementation of *sampleC* will demonstrate how one can check break and continue by means of a separate stack; in general a certain amount of ingenuity is required, since these problems do not fit a uniform framework.

5.2 Symbol table principles

A symbol table is the central place in which the compiler keeps all information associated with user-defined names and constants. While the design of a symbol table entry depends on the information required by the compiler and obtainable from the declarations in a program, the organization of the entries for searching reflects the scope rules of the language:

Basic, for example, can be handled with a table to which each new name is simply added. All names are globally known; thus the table never needs to be pruned unless the entire information about a program is erased. Parameters for user-defined functions are only known within the function; they can be entered into a second table, which is erased as soon as work on the function has been completed.

Fortran essentially requires two tables: one table contains information about all identifiers introduced within a subprogram, while a second table might be used to store subprogram names. The first table would be erased after compilation of each subprogram unit. The second table is not really required if subprograms are combined with a linker; in this case the subprogram names would be reported to the linker.

Pascal has a strict *declare before use* rule and nested scopes. The nested scopes are reflected by using a stack as a symbol table: new names are pushed on top of the stack, and the stack is appropriately popped once the end of a scope, i.e., the end of a function or procedure definition, is reached. Whenever a name is referenced, we can search the stack top-down and thus locate the innermost definition for the name.

Other members of the Algol family do not necessarily require that names be declared before use, as long as a declaration is present *within* the scope of the name. This situation is somewhat involved: we need two passes over a program, the first one to collect all declarations and to essentially propagate them to the beginning of their scope, and the second one to then deal with references based on the information collected in the first pass.

C permits nested scopes for variables, but functions cannot be nested. There is a *declare before use* rule, except that functions with int result need not be declared. In general, a stack of names will do, as long as we keep functions in a global table, even if references to them are discovered locally.

What information is stored in a symbol table entry? For searching purposes, the entry must have access to the user-defined name; for usage verification we must represent the type of the object; and during code generation we will need to store information about the representation of the object — location on a stack, offset or absolute address, length, etc. If the symbol table is organized as a stack, the entries will be linked; if the stack is popped, we need to remember at which scope nesting level the entry was defined.

Representing the type of an object might be difficult. In Fortran there is only a small number of types, and additionally the object can be dimensioned as an array; this can be represented with a few integer values in the symbol table. In languages such as Pascal or C, with a rich set of data type constructors, a recursive description will have to be built, which will usually involve pointers to further symbol table entries.

Name searching is another area where a number of different techniques are available. In general, when the lexical analysis function has assembled a user-defined name or literal constant, it will immediately locate it in the symbol table, or enter it there if it is as yet unknown. From then on, a pointer to the symbol table entry is passed along providing access to information about the symbol, and eliminating the need to *search* the symbol table more then once. The initial search is thus performed by a routine which is called only from the lexical analyzer; in order to speed up this search, data structures such as hash tables might be used in addition to the symbol table itself. Since a lexical analyzer spends a significant amount of processing time on the name search, a lot of literature is available on the subject of table searching; for starters consult, e.g., chapter 3.D. by W. McKeeman in [Bau76].

5.3 Example

For *sampleC* we stick with a symbol table stack, represented as a linear list of entries. In order to keep things as simple as possible, we will not use additional data structures to speed up searching — this is left as an exercise. We manage the entries dynamically using the `calloc()` and `cfree()` library routines.

We will search the symbol table stack backwards from newest to oldest symbol. In this fashion, the innermost declaration of a name will be found first, provided that we pop local entries off the stack once we leave a compound statement.

We therefore need to know where the local declarations of each open block begin. This could be done by a stack of open block descriptors, from which a linked list connects the relevant symbol table entries. To simplify, at the expense of some processing time during block closure, we maintain a global counter of nesting depth of compound statements, and copy the current value of this counter into each symbol table entry when a declaration for the symbol is performed. Local entries on the symbol table stack then are precisely those which were marked with the current nesting depth. Defective programs may result in some symbols never being declared; they are marked with an initialization value for the depth field and are also removed at block closure.

One complication arises from the fact that functions need not be defined before they are used. However, functions may not be nested, so this problem can be solved by moving function descriptors in the symbol table to the outermost block. In our dynamically linked scheme, this is quite easy to accomplish: we simply relink a function descriptor at the bottom of the symbol table stack. We do need to save function descriptors, since we are building a one pass, load-and-go compiler, which does not employ a linker for image assembly, and which therefore must itself check that all referenced functions have actually been defined.

Another, smaller complication is the fact that in C parameters need not be explicitly declared: once their names have been mentioned in a parameter list, they become int variables by default. This can be handled by chaining the parameters in the symbol table, when they are initially found in the parameter_list. Once the parameter_declarations have been reduced, we can follow the chain and default all remaining, undeclared parameters.

While it is not required, we will check consistent use of functions, i.e., we will at least count that they are always called with the same number of arguments.

There is one massive simplification in *sampleC*: since the language only supports an int data type, we need not worry about type incompatibilities. In general, semantic restrictions need to be enforced in this context; this is best done by computing result types as the various operations are recognized by the parser, and by passing the result types along on the *yacc* stack. The resulting analysis is bulky enough so that we decided to omit it here by not supporting additional data types.

First we design a symbol table entry and define possible values for certain fields. This information is placed into *symtab.h*:

```
/*
 *      sample c -- header file for symbol table
 */

struct symtab {
        char *  s_name;            /* name pointer */
        int     s_type;            /* symbol type */
        int     s_blknum:          /* static block depth */
        union {                    /* multi-purpose */
                int s__num;
                struct symtab * s__link;
                } s__;
        int     s_offset;          /* symbol definition */
        struct symtab * s_next;    /* next entry */
        };

#define s_pnum  s__.s__num         /* count of parameters */
#define NOT_SET (-1)               /* no count yet set */
#define s_plist s__.s__link        /* chain of parameters */

/*
 *      s_type values
 */

#define UDEC    0          /* not declared */
#define FUNC    1          /* function */
```

```
#define UFUNC    2       /* undefined function */
#define VAR      3       /* declared variable */
#define PARM     4       /* undeclared parameter */


/*
 *      s_type values for S_TRACE
 */

#define SYMmap  "undeclared", "function", "undefined function", \
                "variable", "parameter"


/*
 *      typed functions, symbol table module
 */

struct symtab * link_parm();    /* chain parameters */
struct symtab * s_find();       /* locate symbol by name */
struct symtab * make_parm();    /* declare parameter */
struct symtab * make_var();     /* define variable */
struct symtab * make_func();    /* define function */


/*
 *      typed library functions
 */

char * strsave();               /* dynamically save a string */
char * calloc();                /* dynamically obtain memory */
```

s_name will be used in the name search. We will use strsave() to dynamically save each new name as a string. s_blknum contains the nesting depth of the scope at which the name was defined. s_offset will later reflect run-time access to an object; currently, it could be omitted. s_next links the elements of the symbol table into a stack.

s__ does double duty. The variant s__link, for convenience defined as s_plist, is used to link all parameters of a function together, so that we may easily default undeclared parameters. For function names the variant s__num, defined as s_pnum, is used to check consistent use: initially it has the value NOT_SET there. Once a function is defined or referenced for the first time (indicated by the value being NOT_SET), s_pnum is set to the number of arguments or parameters specified at this point. Each further reference (indicated by the value being different from NOT_SET) can then be investigated.

s_type, finally, must represent the type of the symbol table entry. This component is oversimplified — as soon as pointers and vectors (let alone structures) are added to the language, a much more complicated representation will have to be designed. At present, very little is required: a name is initially entered as undeclared (UDEC); if the name is referenced but not yet defined as a function, s_type is set to UFUNC; once the function is defined, this value is changed to FUNC; alternatively, a name may refer to a parameter (PARM) or to a variable (VAR), either of which can only be an integer.

For tracing purposes, we will dump the symbol table. Rather then displaying numerical representations of s_type, we maintain SYMmap in parallel to the numerical representations. The encoding is a potential hazard to safe modification of the symbol table routines, but at least we have placed the two representations in close proximity to each other.

As another point on programming style, note that we followed a silent convention in starting all component names of the symbol table entry structure with the same prefix s_.

Following the technique employed for the formatter, we again place all symbol table utilities in a separate file, *symtab.c*. The grammar is extended with actions calling on these utilities for semantic tests. Basically, for *sampleC* every occurrence of Identifier has to be checked. break and continue should also be checked — we chose to defer this problem until code generation so that we can deal with the problem of implementing the appropriate jumps at the same time.

Rather then discussing actions added to the grammar and symbol table utilities separately, we will describe the additions to the parser and the utility functions in parallel. This is our actual sequence of implementation: using the grammar rules as a guide, we consider each occurrence of Identifier in turn, decide what needs to be checked, add a call on a utility function as an action to the formulation, and implement the utility function in *symtab.c*. The table nature of the grammar ensures that we consider all possible cases; the grammar serves as an ideal control structure guiding the implementation process. Section 4 in the appendix can be consulted for a listing of all the utility functions together.

We begin by defining the necessary global variables. Since they are the exclusive property of the symbol table manager, they are defined to be static; in this fashion *symtab.c* hides its private data from the other modules of the compiler. Similarly, we only export from this module — by not specifying the static attribute to the global name — those functions which are actually called from the actions in the parser module. All internal utilities are hidden as static objects.

```
        /*
         *      sample c -- symbol table definition and manipulation
         */

        #include "symtab.h"
        #include "y.tab.h"

        /*
         *      symbol table
         */

        static  struct  symtab
                symtab,                 /* blind element */
                * s_gbl;                /* global end of chain */
        #define s_lcl   (& symtab)      /* local end of chain */

        /*
         *      block table
         */

        static int blknum = 0;          /* current static block depth */
```

The symbol table has the following dynamic structure:

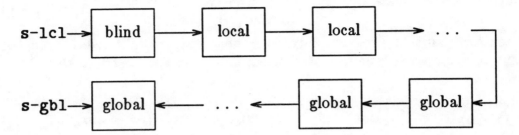

s_lcl points to a blind element, which never changes, and after which new entries are added. Along the chain, at the bottom of the stack, are the global entries, which are essentially never popped. The function s_create() will add a new, local entry to the symbol table for the name given as an argument. The new entry is marked as being undeclared.

```
static struct symtab * s_create(name)
        register char * name;
{       register struct symtab * new_entry = (struct symtab *)
                        calloc(1, sizeof(struct symtab));

        if (new_entry)
        {       new_entry->s_next = s_lcl->s_next;
                s_lcl->s_next = new_entry;
                new_entry->s_name = strsave(name);
                new_entry->s_type = UDEC;
                new_entry->s_blknum = 0;
                new_entry->s_pnum = NOT_SET;
                return new_entry;
        }
        fatal("No more room for symbols.");
        /*NOTREACHED*/
}
```

s_gbl marks the *last* (lowest) global element; if a function description is moved to the global end of the chain, it is moved to follow s_gbl, and s_gbl is then pointed to it. This is accomplished by the routine s_move() which has as an argument a pointer to the entry to be moved:

```
static s_move(symbol)
        register struct symtab * symbol;
{       register struct symtab * ptr;

        /* find desired entry in symtab chain (bug if missing) */
        for (ptr = s_lcl; ptr->s_next != symbol; ptr = ptr->s_next)
                if (! ptr->s_next)
                        bug("s_move");

        /* unlink it from its present position */
        ptr->s_next = symbol->s_next;

        /* relink at global end of symtab */
        s_gbl->s_next = symbol;
        s_gbl = symbol;
```

```
        s_gbl->s_next = (struct symtab *) 0;
}
```

Note that the entry is only linked into a different position on the symbol table stack; the entry itself is not moved in memory, so the pointer value referencing the element and passed as an argument does not change.

We placed a blind element on top of the symbol table stack, so that we do not need to check if we are moving the current top of the stack, i.e., so that we do not need to adjust s_lcl as a special case.

Initially, however, s_gbl may not point at the blind element — if it did, we would add the first (global) definition *following* s_gbl, local definitions might get positioned *between* s_gbl and this global definition, eventually one of them might be moved to become global... and general mayhem would result! s_gbl must be initialized to point to a global entry — a blind element there would split the symbol table into two halves and would thus create another special case. Fortunately, there is a useful global entry: every *sampleC* program must contain a main() function — initially, we therefore open the outermost block, and initialize s_gbl to point to an entry for main as an undefined function:

```
init()
{
        blk_push();
        s_gbl = s_create("main");
        s_gbl->s_type = UFUNC;
}
```

init() must be called before the symbol table can be accessed. A call to init() therefore can be placed into the main() function of our compiler, prior to the call to yyparse(). Another, more visible solution is to call init() very early from the parser itself. This is the first action added to the parser:

```
program
        :               { init(); }
            definitions
                { blk_pop(); }
```

In this fashion, init() will be called before any calls to the lexical analyzer.

init() pushes the block stack:

```
blk_push()
{
        ++ blknum;
}
```

Every call to blk_push() must be balanced by a call to blk_pop() to pop henceforth inaccessible symbols from the symbol table stack, to discover undefined functions, etc. We will defer a discussion of blk_pop() until we have seen how symbols are actually entered into the symbol table.

Every user-defined name is first seen by the lexical analyzer. yylex() must enter every symbol into the symbol table, as long as it is not already there. We have already placed calls to a function s_lookup() into the lexical analyzer for this purpose; s_lookup() is called with the terminal symbol representation in yytext[] and with

the desired terminal symbol value, Constant or Identifier, as an argument. For
sampleC it is sufficient to dynamically save the text of a Constant. An Identifier
must be located or entered in the symbol table:

```
s_lookup(yylex)
        int yylex;              /* Constant or Identifier */
{       extern char yytext[];   /* text of symbol */

        switch (yylex) {
        case Constant:
                yylval.y_str = strsave(yytext);
                break;
        case Identifier:
                if (yylval.y_sym = s_find(yytext))
                        break;
                yylval.y_sym = s_create(yytext);
                break;
        default:
                bug("s_lookup");
        }
}
```

In either case, yylval subsequently contains a pointer which provides access to the
semantic information for the user-defined terminal symbol. While we know that
s_lookup() will not be called with an argument other than Constant or Integer, we
verify the argument value as a matter of robust coding.

We have deferred the problem of locating an entry in the symbol table by name.
This is one of the less efficient routines in this implementation:

```
struct symtab * s_find(name)
        char * name;
{       register struct symtab * ptr;

        /* search symtab until match or end of symtab chain */
        for (ptr = s_lcl->s_next; ptr; ptr = ptr->s_next)
                if (! ptr->s_name)
                        bug("s_find");
                else
                        /* return ptr if names match */
                        if (strcmp(ptr->s_name, name) == 0)
                                return ptr;
        /* search fails, return NULL */
        return (struct symtab *) 0;
}
```

Using s_lookup(), yylex() has made arrangements for every Identifier to be
present in the symbol table. A new entry is UDEC, but if the name has been seen previously, yylval may or may not point to the proper entry. We need to repair or check
things wherever Identifier appears in the grammar.

Since names in C — with the exception of function names — must be declared
before they are used, declarations will be reduced first. Consider therefore the point
where an Identifier appears in a parameter_list, i.e., where an Identifier
becomes a new parameter:

```
parameter_list
        : Identifier
                { $$ = link_parm($1, 0); }
        | parameter_list ',' Identifier
                { $$ = link_parm($3, $1);
                  yyerrok;
                }
        | error
                { $$ = 0; }
        | parameter_list error
        | parameter_list error Identifier
                { $$ = link_parm($3, $1);
                  yyerrok;
                }
        | parameter_list ',' error
```

link_parm() and the *yacc* value stack are used to form a chain of all parameter names in this parameter_list. link_parm() is also given the responsibility of reflecting the Identifier as a PARM in the symbol table. Later we will use the parameter chain to give undeclared parameters a default and to count the number of parameters. Let us first look at link_parm():

```
struct symtab * link_parm(symbol, next)
        register struct symtab * symbol, * next;
{
        switch (symbol->s_type) {
        case PARM:
                error("duplicate parameter %s", symbol->s_name);
                return next;
        case FUNC:
        case UFUNC:
        case VAR:
                symbol = s_create(symbol->s_name);
        case UDEC:
                break;
        default:
                bug("link_parm");
        }
        symbol->s_type = PARM;
        symbol->s_blknum = blknum;
        symbol->s_plist = next;
        return symbol;
}
```

yylex() located the Identifier already in the symbol table and this entry is passed to link_parm(). The s_type field of this entry determines what needs to be done:

If the entry is UDEC, it is a new name and can itself be defined to be a parameter.

If the entry is typed but is not a PARM, it refers to a global Identifier which is about to be hidden by a parameter. We must therefore create a new, local symbol table entry for the same name with s_create(), which is automatically pushed on top of the symbol table stack and thus hides the global entry. The local entry can then be defined to be a PARM.

If the entry is already a PARM, we must complain about the same name being used as a parameter twice in the same parameter list.

The link_parm() function was relatively easy to design: the grammar isolates the context of this part of the semantic analysis, and the possible values of the s_type component of the entry in the symbol table prompt us to consider all possible cases. Since C does not permit function nesting, the situation is relatively simple to handle.

Declaring a parameter is slightly more complicated. This happens when Identifier is found in parameter_declarator_list:

```
parameter_declarator_list
        : Identifier
                { make_parm($1); }
        | parameter_declarator_list ',' Identifier
                { make_parm($3);
                  yyerrok;
                }
        | error
        | parameter_declarator_list error
        | parameter_declarator_list error Identifier
                { make_parm($3);
                  yyerrok;
                }
        | parameter_declarator_list ',' error
```

make_parm() must change PARM in the symbol table into VAR, thus declaring the parameter. Once the parameter_declarations have been taken care of, we will need to declare all remaining PARM entries as integer variables, i.e., as VAR, too.

make_parm() is presented with the symbol table entry, which yylex() found or created through s_lookup(). If we again consider all possible values for s_type in this entry, we discover various possibilities for errors:

If the entry is already marked as VAR, and if this happened at nesting level two, we have two declarations for the same parameter. This is different from the same name occurring in the parameter *list* twice.

If VAR stems from a different nesting level (hopefully global!), or if we find any other value except PARM, we must complain about an attempt to declare as a parameter a name which was not specified in the parameter_list. For safety, we again create a new, duplicate entry for the name and declare it as a VAR.

```
struct symtab * make_parm(symbol)
        register struct symtab * symbol;
{
        switch (symbol->s_type) {
        case VAR:
                if (symbol->s_blknum == 2)
                {       error("parameter %s declared twice",
                                symbol->s_name);
                        return symbol;
                }
        case UDEC:
        case FUNC:
        case UFUNC:
                error("%s is not a parameter", symbol->s_name);
```

```
                symbol = s_create(symbol->s_name);
        case PARM:
                break;
        default:
                bug("make_parm");
        }
        symbol->s_type = VAR;
        symbol->s_blknum = blknum;
        return symbol;
}
```

We turn to defining a variable. This happens in a grammatical context which is identical to the declaration of parameters. However, the necessary semantic actions are quite different. We therefore specify separate grammatical rules for variable definitions and parameter declarations; if we extend *sampleC* in the direction of C, we need to make the distinction anyhow: variables may be initialized, parameters may not.

```
declarator_list
        : Identifier
                { make_var($1); }
        | declarator_list ',' Identifier
                { make_var($3);
                  yyerrok;
                }
        | error
        | declarator_list error
        | declarator_list error Identifier
                { make_var($3);
                  yyerrok;
                }
        | declarator_list ',' error
```

make_var() is given the responsibility of reflecting the definition in the symbol table. Its argument again references the symbol table entry which yylex() has found. This entry has one of the values defined for s_type; each case is again considered individually:

If the entry is undeclared, we have a new name which we define to be a variable in the current block.

If the entry references a function or a variable in the same block, we will complain about a name being defined twice. Otherwise we need to duplicate the symbol table entry using s_create(), so that we obtain a local entry, which we can then define as required.

Additionally we must guard against the case of a local variable having the same name as a parameter. The parameter at this point is a VAR, but as we shall see below, it is at nesting level two, while the local variable would be at level three. This is a special case which cannot happen for functions.

Lastly, we should not be able to find a PARM entry, since they have all either been declared or defaulted. To guard against evil input errors, we provide an error message in this case, too.

```
struct symtab * make_var(symbol)
        register struct symtab * symbol;
{
        switch (symbol->s_type) {
        case VAR:
        case FUNC:
        case UFUNC:
                if (symbol->s_blknum == blknum
                    || symbol->s_blknum == 2 && blknum == 3)
                        error("duplicate name %s", symbol->s_name);
                symbol = s_create(symbol->s_name);
        case UDEC:
                break;
        case PARM:
                error("unexpected parameter %s", symbol->s_name);
                break;
        default:
                bug("make_var");
        }
        symbol->s_type = VAR;
        symbol->s_blknum = blknum;
        return symbol;
}
```

This routine must cope with most aspects of block structure. Still, what needs to be considered is enumerated by the possible values for s_type and the nesting levels at which we may encounter those values in a previously entered symbol.

We have already discovered a few tasks to be accomplished when defining a function: the length of the parameter_list must be computed and checked or entered into the function definition, and we must manage the nesting level for parameters properly. This last problem is handled with an additional pair of calls to blk_push() and blk_pop() surrounding the parameter manipulations. Consider a function definition in the grammar:

```
function_definition
        : Identifier '('
                { make_func($1); blk_push(); }
          optional_parameter_list rp
          declarations
                { chk_parm($1, parm_default($4)); }
          compound_statement
                { blk_pop(); }

optional_parameter_list
        : /* null */
                { $$ = 0;   /* no formal parameters */ }
        | parameter_list
                /* $$ = $1 = chain of formal parameters */
```

make_func() must define the function in the symbol table. chk_parm() is given a pointer to the symbol table entry for the function and the number of parameters specified; the routine must check if all is well, or set the number of parameters on first access. parm_default() is an action which deals with all those parameters which were mentioned in the parameter_list but not declared in the parameter declarations. In

C, those parameters must be defaulted to be `int` variables; they must be `PARM` and we declare them to be `VAR`. `parm_default()` additionally must count the parameters and return their number. Consider the functions in turn:

```
struct symtab * make_func(symbol)
        register struct symtab * symbol;
{

        switch (symbol->s_type) {
        case UFUNC:
        case UDEC:
                break;
        case VAR:
                error("function name %s same as global variable",
                        symbol->s_name);
                return symbol;
        case FUNC:
                error("duplicate function definition %s",
                        symbol->s_name);
                return symbol;
        default:
                bug("make_func");
        }
        symbol->s_type = FUNC;
        symbol->s_blknum = 1;
        return symbol;

}
```

When `make_func()` is called, we are at the global nesting level and do not need to move a symbol table entry. A `UDEC` or `UFUNC` entry can simply be defined as a function, a `VAR` or `FUNC` is about to be duplicated, and nothing else can legitimately be encountered.

At this point, `make_var()`, `make_parm()`, and `make_func()` need not return result values. However, once we start code generation, we will need the correct symbol table pointers so that we can add information such as the location of a variable or the starting address of a function. This is why these three functions have been designed to return the corrected symbol table pointer. If something goes wrong, e.g., if we encounter duplicate definitions, not much can be salvaged. A compiler is not required to be clairvoyant, it is only expected not to crash even under the user's most inconsiderate approach.

Checking or setting the parameter count is very simple:

```
chk_parm(symbol, count)
        register struct symtab * symbol;
        register int count;
{

        if (symbol->s_pnum == NOT_SET)
                symbol->s_pnum = count;
        else if ((int) symbol->s_pnum != count)
                warning("function %s should have %d argument(s)",
                        symbol->s_name, symbol->s_pnum);
}
```

Defaulting undeclared parameters is just as easy. We merely need to follow the chain through the symbol table:

```
int parm_default(symbol)
        register struct symtab * symbol;
{       register int count = 0;

        while (symbol)
        {       ++ count;
                if (symbol->s_type == PARM)
                        symbol->s_type = VAR;
                symbol = symbol->s_plist;
        }
        return count;
}
```

Almost the grand finale: having entered the symbols into the symbol table, we will now consider how to evict them during block closure. blk_pop() is called for the global block from the action associated with program, for the parameter block from an action associated with the function definition, and lastly from an action associated with compound_statement:

```
compound_statement
        : '{'
                { blk_push(); }
          declarations statements rr
                { blk_pop(); }
```

We need a loop which will traverse the current nesting level in the symbol table, so that we may unlink and free all local entries. If we find undefined entries, we have usually complained about them before; however, undefined functions will be found once we free the global block.

```
blk_pop()
{       register struct symtab * ptr;

        for (ptr = s_lcl->s_next;
                ptr &&
                (ptr->s_blknum >= blknum || ptr->s_blknum == 0);
                ptr = s_lcl->s_next)
        {
                if (! ptr->s_name)
                        bug("blk_pop null name");
#ifdef TRACE
        {       static char * type[] = { SYMmap };

                message("Popping %s: %s, depth %d, offset %d",
                        ptr->s_name, type[ptr->s_type],
                        ptr->s_blknum, ptr->s_offset);
        }
#endif TRACE
                if (ptr->s_type == UFUNC)
                        error("undefined function %s",
                                ptr->s_name);
                cfree(ptr->s_name);
                s_lcl->s_next = ptr->s_next;
```

```
                        cfree(ptr);
            }
            -- blknum;
    }
```

We must ignore the initial blind element, we must not follow a null pointer out of the symbol table — actually we should not find such a pointer — and we must consider all entries with the current nesting level, hopefully `blknum`. A few entries at nesting level zero, i.e., uninitialized entries, can also be encountered — they result for example from symbols dropped during error recovery. Yes — we will encounter symbols which our reducing actions never had a shot at!

`blk_pop()` is a good place to provide some tracing output so that we can see what is happening. We have conditionally inserted instructions to print all components of a symbol table entry as it is freed.

So far we have gone to great lengths to enter information into the symbol table. We must now make use of it: whenever an `Identifier` is used in a formulation, we need to compare the symbol table entry with the context to see if the use is legitimate. In *sampleC* there are only two essential situations to consider. One is this:

```
binary
        : Identifier
                { chk_var($1); }
        | PP Identifier
                { chk_var($2); }
        | Identifier '=' binary
                { chk_var($1); }
```

(We have omitted a number of very similar formulations here.)

`chk_var()` must determine whether the `Identifier` passed as an argument can be referenced as a variable on either side of an assignment. Once again, the various values of `s_type` will provide the answer:

```
chk_var(symbol)
        register struct symtab * symbol;
{
        switch (symbol->s_type) {
        case UDEC:
                error("undeclared variable %s", symbol->s_name);
                break;
        case PARM:
                error("unexpected parameter %s", symbol->s_name);
                break;
        case FUNC:
        case UFUNC:
                error("function %s used as variable",
                        symbol->s_name);
        case VAR:
                return;
        default:
                bug("check_var");
        }
        symbol->s_type = VAR;
        symbol->s_blknum = blknum;
```

```
        }
```

Observe that we protect ourselves from a cascade of error messages about the same undefined variable or parameter which we missed: if we find one, we complain about it once and then define it in the current block. In this way we avoid subsequent complaints. This explains why a loop traversing the current nesting level in the symbol table might encounter block numbers strictly greater than the current block number: they can result from such a repair.

The last test concerns the use of an Identifier as a function name in a function call. We also check the number of arguments using the chk_parm() function developed earlier. This time, however, we need to count the number of arguments:

```
        binary
                : Identifier '('
                        { chk_func($1); }
                  optional_argument_list rp
                        { chk_parm($1,$4); }

        optional_argument_list
                : /* null */
                        { $$ = 0;   /* # of actual arguments */ }
                | argument_list
                        /* $$ = $1 = # of actual arguments */

        argument_list
                : binary
                        { $$ = 1; }
                | argument_list ',' binary
                        { ++ $$;
                          yyerrok;
                        }
                | error
                        { $$ = 0; }
                | argument_list error
                | argument_list ',' error
```

Here is chk_func(), the last of the symbol table utilities:

```
        chk_func(symbol)
                register struct symtab * symbol;
        {
                switch (symbol->s_type) {
                case UDEC:
                        break;
                case PARM:
                        error("unexpected parameter %s", symbol->s_name);
                        symbol->s_pnum = NOT_SET;
                        return;
                case VAR:
                        error("variable %s used as function",
                                symbol->s_name);
                        symbol->s_pnum = NOT_SET;
                case UFUNC:
                case FUNC:
                        return;
```

```
        default:
                bug("check_func");
        }
        s_move(symbol);
        symbol->s_type = UFUNC;
        symbol->s_blknum = 1;

}
```

If we find a new name in the position of a function name during a call, the name is implicitly defined to be a function name. In this case we must relocate its entry in the symbol table, a task accomplished by s_move(), and must mark it to be an undeclared, globally nested function.

If there were no previous input errors, we should not be able to find a parameter. If we find one anyway, we make sure that a subsequent call to chk_parm() will not provoke a message: we pretend that the number of parameters for this "function" is NOT_SET. Variables misused as functions are similarly protected.

This completes the symbol table facilities. We have tacitly assumed the existence of a few routines to issue various error and warning messages:

message()

issues an unadorned message with a position indication produced by yywhere(); see section 3.3.

warning()

issues a message and identifies it as a warning.

error()

issues a message, identifying and counting it as an error.

fatal()

issues a message, identifies it as a fatal error, and terminates the process. This routine is called if the compiler runs out of resources (memory), or is otherwise incapable of completing the compilation.

bug()

should "never" happen. A message is issued, identified as a bug, and the process is terminated. This routine is only called in situations which must not happen if the compiler was produced correctly. We prefer to issue a brief message — if the bug is actually encountered, we would then attempt to recompile the compiler with a more informative message and see what we find. While this reduces the size of the production compiler, in really bad cases the recompiled compiler might not reproduce the bug.

All these routines are called just like the library function printf() with a format and a varying, small number of values to be displayed. The routines are shown in section 3 of the appendix.

Consider the following program which deliberately contains a number of errors:

```
/*
 *      symtab demonstration, including errors
 */
```

```
main(a,b) int a,b;
{       a=b;
        {a;b;}
        if (a==b) {a;b;}
        if (a==b+1) a; else b;
        while (a==b) {a; break;}
        return;
}
int f() { int x; int y; return x+y; }
f(a,b)                   /* 14: duplicate function definition */
        int a;          /* undeclared parm b (not an error) */
{       int b,c;        /* 16: symbol b duplicates parm b */
        int c,d;        /* 17: duplicate symbol c */
        e=b;            /* 18: undeclared e */
        f=c+d;          /* 19: use func for var */
        a(b);           /* 20: use var for func */
        g();            /* 21: undefined function g */
}
h(a,a)                   /* 23: duplicate parameter */
        int f;          /* 24: not a parameter */
        int a;
        int a;          /* 26: duplicate parameter */
{ }
```

Syntax and semantic analysis of this program result in the following messages (assuming TRACE is defined):

```
line 12 near "}": Popping b: variable, depth 2, offset 0
line 12 near "}": Popping a: variable, depth 2, offset 0
line 13 near "}": Popping y: variable, depth 3, offset 0
line 13 near "}": Popping x: variable, depth 3, offset 0
[error 1] line 14 near "(": duplicate function definition f
[warning] line 16 near "{": function f should have 0 argument(s)
[error 2] line 16 near "b": duplicate name b
[error 3] line 17 near "c": duplicate name c
[error 4] line 18 near ";": undeclared variable e
[error 5] line 19 near ";": function f used as variable
[error 6] line 20 near "(": variable a used as function
line 22 near "}": Popping e: variable, depth 3, offset 0
line 22 near "}": Popping d: variable, depth 3, offset 0
line 22 near "}": Popping c: variable, depth 3, offset 0
line 22 near "}": Popping c: variable, depth 3, offset 0
line 22 near "}": Popping b: variable, depth 3, offset 0
line 22 near "}": Popping b: variable, depth 2, offset 0
line 22 near "}": Popping a: variable, depth 2, offset 0
[error 7] line 23 near "a": duplicate parameter a
[error 8] line 24 near "f": f is not a parameter
[error 9] line 26 near "a": parameter a declared twice
line 27 near "}": Popping f: variable, depth 2, offset 0
line 27 near "}": Popping a: variable, depth 2, offset 0
line 27: Popping h: function, depth 1, offset 0
line 27: Popping f: function, depth 1, offset 0
line 27: Popping main: function, depth 1, offset 0
line 27: Popping g: undefined function, depth 1, offset 0
[error 10] line 27: undefined function g
```

5.4 Typing the value stack

While implementing the symbol table facilities and semantic checks, we have made heavy use of the value stack: for Identifier terminal symbols, we passed symbol table pointers from the lexical analyzer to the parser; for Constant terminal symbols, we passed pointers to dynamically acquired string storage; we chained the parameter_list using symbol table pointers; and we counted up the number of expressions in the argument_list on the value stack as well. This last use of stack elements unfortunately necessitates a union of types for the value stack. We count using an int variable, but we point to the symbol table using a pointer data type. While pointers in C can be cast as pointers to any data type, it is still a good idea to employ different data type specifications when pointing to strings and to symbol table elements.

Even as a union, the value stack could still be typed as described in section 3.6. However, once we refer to stack elements using the $i syntax within actions, we need to inform *yacc* just what component of the union should be referenced in each case. To put it differently, we must associate a data type syntactically represented as a union component with all those symbols presented to *yacc* which we reference through $i or $$. This of course requires certain extensions of the *yacc* specification syntax described up to now.

We prefer to "type" our grammar in a separate editing pass following construction of all the actions. During this pass we need to note all terminal *and* non-terminal symbols which are referenced on the value stack and decide on a data type for the corresponding value stack element. If we rely on the default action

```
    { $$ = $1; }
```

to actually pass a value, we need to consider the associated symbols even if the default action is not explicitly specified. (This is one reason why we usually comment those points in a *yacc* specification in which we rely on the default action.)

Once all the necessary data types are known together with those symbols which need to be typed, we can proceed to modify the *yacc* specification. We will describe the modification using the *sampleC* specification as a concrete example.

First we must define the data type of value stack elements. This is done in the first part of the *yacc* specification using a union declaration in the style of C, prefixed by a % character[1]. In our case, value stack elements can be pointers to the symbol table, pointers to character strings, and integer values for counting. We define:

```
%union  {
        struct symtab * y_sym;    /* Identifier */
        char * y_str;             /* Constant */
        int y_num;                /* count */
        }
```

---

[1] There are other methods to define the data type, but we believe this technique to be both visible in the *yacc* specification, and convenient, since the resulting union declaration as well as an extern declaration for yylval are automatically placed into the file *y.tab.h*.

Next we type those terminal symbols for which during lexical analysis a value is assigned to yylval. Syntactically, this is achieved by placing the name of a union component, enclosed in angle brackets, between %token and the list of terminal names to be so typed. In our case, Identifier and Constant have corresponding values on the stack:

```
%token   <y_sym> Identifier
%token   <y_str> Constant
```

The values are assigned to yylval by the routine s_lookup(). These assignments must, of course, also use union components — this has already been tacitly done correctly in section 5.3.

Finally we must type all those non-terminal symbols for which $i or $$ are referenced. This is accomplished by making a %type definition in a manner very similar to a %token definition for terminal symbols. We must type argument_list and optional_argument_list for counting purposes, and parameter_list and optional_parameter_list to pass the parameter chain header:

```
%type    <y_sym> optional_parameter_list, parameter_list
%type    <y_num> optional_argument_list, argument_list
```

It should be noted that as soon as %union, %type, or the < > syntax is used, *yacc* very strictly checks that *all* references to the value stack are typed appropriately. Any omission immediately causes *yacc* to terminate with a fatal error indicating the offending line in the specification.

One subtle typing facility, required especially for anonymous non-terminal symbols (see section 3.7), has not yet been discussed. It will be shown when it is required in section 6.2.

5.5 Problems

1. Write a *sampleC* test program containing deliberate errors to provoke all semantic error messages in the compiler.

2. Change the method of storing symbols for *sampleC* to use a hash scheme, to speed up the search for names. Demonstrate, e.g., using the C profiling option, that there is a gain in efficiency.

3. Add to *sampleC* a block descriptor stack, which can essentially be maintained as part of the *yacc* value stack. What changes will this require in typing of the value stack? Again, try to measure the gain in efficiency.

4. Remove those parts of symbol table management which will be unnecessary if a linking loader is used. Decide how (and when) to pass information to the linker.

5. Extend the desk calculator with simple string operations. Use the operator + to denote both addition and string concatenation. Should the resulting problem be handled in the grammar, or by separate semantic routines? I.e., should the grammar know Constant, or rather Number and String?

Chapter 6
Memory Allocation

We are now ready to define an *implementation* of the *sampleC* language for a particular machine. We must develop policies for *memory allocation* and *code generation*.

It is interesting to note that the entire problem of language recognition could be solved without any knowledge of the target machine. This serves to emphasize that a significant amount of the code of a compiler can be completely target- and host-machine independent.

In this and the following chapters, we will emphasize the principles rather than attempt to cope with the peculiarities of a particular machine. We will therefore describe the implementation for a fictitious machine which is adapted to the requirements of the *sampleC* source language.

6.1 Principles

The memory allocation policy defines the representation of variables, i.e., the implementation of declarations. We must decide how much memory to allocate to an object of each data type, and how to address the object, i.e., where to place it during program execution, to support particular life expectancies.

Run time memory assignment tends to mirror symbol table organization to some extent. Consider:

In Basic, there are only global variables, kept in a global symbol table, which for an interpreter might as well also hold the values of the variables during execution. The parameters of user-defined functions can be handled with the same stack which is normally used for expression evaluation.

In Fortran, subprograms cannot be called recursively. Since the values of local variables must be preserved between successive calls to the same function, we must assign a unique memory cell for each variable in each subprogram.

In C, Pascal, and other Algol-like languages, subprograms can be called recursively; hence, we must dynamically allocate space for the local variables of a subprogram as it is called. Since local variables normally cease to exist once a subprogram terminates, we can free and reuse their space. Function invocation is a stack discipline, and this discipline must be employed for managing the local variables as well.

The nesting of scopes in Algol-like languages poses an additional problem. If functions may be nested during definition, they have access by name only to a selective subset of the local variables of the currently activated functions.

The nesting of compound statements, with the associated rules for the life expectancy of variables declared within a compound statement, leads to a reuse of memory which can be managed at compile time. Compound statements can be viewed as anonymous subprograms which can only be entered sequentially, i.e., in the same order as the compiler sees them. Since compound statements are anonymous, they can themselves not be called recursively; thus, the compiler has full information about the behavior of the life expectancy of local variables defined in a compound statement.

Representing scalar data types tends to be simple — they usually reflect particular objects for which a direct machine representation and associated operations exist. Enumeration data types, found, e.g., in Pascal or C, are a rare exception.

Representing data structures is much harder. Vectors or arrays as language elements require that some address arithmetic be performed by the compiler and some at run time, and in a language like APL, they even necessitate elaborate dynamic memory management. Matters are still relatively simple if arrays have fixed, constant bounds as in Pascal, or at least cannot be dynamically dimensioned as in Fortran or C. In this case, the compiler can make arrangements for allocation, i.e., for address assignment — arrays then behave just like very big scalar objects. If arrays can be dynamically dimensioned, as in PL/I, their allocation can only be completed at run time. At this point, they are usually handled through pointers.

Unless case-variant records are really implemented with varying memory requirements, as suggested by the Pascal definition, records and structures are relatively easy to implement. Addresses for the components must be assigned relative to the origin of the structure, and alignment problems must be guarded against. Following that, structures as a whole behave like large scalar objects.

Pointers, although "a step backwards, from which we may never recover" (C. A. R. Hoare), are simply represented as machine addresses. Trouble with pointers results from the fact that as a matter of semantics, they are usually restricted to point to objects of a specific data type. While the usage can be checked at compile time, the validity of values (addresses) stored in pointers is hard to monitor even at run time. The presence of pointers in a language definition usually implies the existence of dynamic memory management. Supporting an allocation function like `calloc()` or `new()` is easy — as a first approximation we just deal out successive pieces of an array — but once an explicit disposal function like `cfree()` or `dispose()` enters the picture, pointers are no longer verifiable with inexpensive means.

Let us now consider the essential aspects of memory allocation for a C-like language in more detail: we must decide on the representation of the data types, on the allocation policy within a nest of compound statements, and on the dynamic allocation of space for nested activation of functions.

For *sampleC* the first decision is simple, since we only have integer variables: each object will take one word of computer memory.

Addressing is more complicated, since we have global and local objects, and since functions may be called recursively. Additionally, there is a significant leniency in parameter passing: the number of formal parameters need not match the number of actual arguments, but the program must function properly as long as only parameters are accessed for which arguments have been passed.

The general solution is to collect local variables for each function into an *activation record* and to maintain at execution time a stack of these records corresponding to function activations. A global activation record can be constructed at code generation time to contain the global variables. During execution, this global activation record is the first entry on the activation record stack.

If we generate code for a stack machine, we can use the machine's stack for activation records, for the evaluation of arithmetic expressions, and for passing arguments to subprograms. Argument values are placed on this stack *prior* to establishing the activation record for the function being called and *in reverse order*, so that their relative offsets at execution time from the beginning of the activation record of the called function are known at code generation time, in spite of the fact that their number is not.

Reversing the order of the arguments is a slight complication which requires intermediate storage of the argument expressions during code generation; "fortunately", our fictitious machine supports (essentially) a separate activation record for parameter passing.

Variables are assigned to activation records by assigning unique offsets, and storing these offsets in the symbol table for later use by the code generation phase. Offsets are defined relative to the beginning of the activation record, and arrangements must be made to have the accessible activation record base addresses available at run time.

For C-like languages we only need three such base addresses, namely for the global activation record, for the parameter region, and for the current local activation record. For Algol-like languages, where function definitions may be nested, access to many activation records may be possible and required at the same time, and the necessary arrangements are somewhat elaborate. Things become even more complicated if functions can be passed as parameters in an Algol-like language: the addresses of the activation records accessible to the function, termed the *display*, are an implicit part of such a parameter function. This is why function calling in Pascal tends to be an expensive operation, while in C it is not.

Once a function call takes place, the old display must be saved (stack-fashion) so that it can be restored when the function returns. The display essentially becomes part of the return address for the function call. For C or *sampleC*, we need to save the address of the previous local activation record, since the global activation record is always accessible.

Like many other languages, *sampleC* permits definitions with reduced scope and life expectancy in nested compound statements. This feature does not result in more activation records to be managed at run time. Instead, we maintain a counter for local offsets across compound statements while collecting an activation record for an entire function at code generation time.

The local offset counter is initialized to zero once a function header is processed. Additionally, a maximum value of this counter will also be maintained. At the beginning of a compound statement, we push the current value of the local offset counter onto a stack. The counter is then incremented as required by each local variable definition. Once the compound statement is completed, the current local offset is compared to the maximum known thus far, and if necessary a new maximum is recorded. Then the local offset counter is restored from its stack to the value at the beginning of the present compound statement. In this fashion, variables declared in two compound statements at the *same* nesting level will occupy the same memory locations (at different times).

When processing of a local activation record is completed, we always know its size, so that we can later generate code to dynamically allocate sufficient amounts of memory.

In C, since global data definitions can be mixed with function definitions, we maintain a separate global offset counter. It is initialized to a suitable value, and is incremented during definition of each global variable.

Parameters are chained during recognition of the parameter list. Declarations for the parameters are collected next — different parameters might require different amounts of space depending on their declaration. Once all parameter declarations for a function have been processed, we can follow the parameter chain and make the actual offset assignments for all parameters together; at this point the order of the chain and the parameter declarations determine order and amount of offsets assigned.

6.2 Example

The following example demonstrates the desired reallocation of parts of the activation record to compound statements at the same level:

```
/*
 *      allocation demonstration -- specifically nested compounds
 */

main(p0, p1)
{       int main0, main1;
        {       int nest2, nest3, nest4;
        }
        {       int new2;
                {       int inner3;
                }
                {       int inner3, inner4;
                }
        }
        {       int last2;
        }
}
```

For this function, we should define the following activation record:

parameter 0	p0		
1	p1		

local	0	main0		
	1	main1		
	2	nest2	new2	last2
	3	nest3	inner3	inner3
	4	nest4		inner4

——— time ——➤

Here is the output from our memory allocator, once this example is processed:

```
line 6 near "{": parameter region has 2 word(s)
line 8 near "}": Popping nest4: variable, depth 4, offset 4
line 8 near "}": Popping nest3: variable, depth 4, offset 3
line 8 near "}": Popping nest2: variable, depth 4, offset 2
line 11 near "}": Popping inner3: variable, depth 5, offset 3
line 13 near "}": Popping inner4: variable, depth 5, offset 4
line 13 near "}": Popping inner3: variable, depth 5, offset 3
line 14 near "}": Popping new2: variable, depth 4, offset 2
line 16 near "}": Popping last2: variable, depth 4, offset 2
line 17 near "}": Popping main1: variable, depth 3, offset 1
line 17 near "}": Popping main0: variable, depth 3, offset 0
line 17 near "}": Popping p1: variable, depth 2, offset 1
line 17 near "}": Popping p0: variable, depth 2, offset 0
line 17 near "}": local region has 5 word(s)
line 17: Popping main: function, depth 1, offset 0
line 17: global region has 1 word(s)
```

This output is produced by the trace installed as part of the symbol table complex: offsets are defined in the s_offset component of a symbol table entry, and this component is shown by the trace.

Let us look at the actions required for memory allocation. An offset in the local or global activation record must be assigned when the variable name is introduced in a declarator_list:

```
declarator_list
        : Identifier
                { all_var($1); }
        | declarator_list ',' Identifier
                { all_var($3);
                    yyerrok;
                }
        | error
        | declarator_list error
        | declarator_list error Identifier
                { all_var($3);
                    yyerrok;
                }
        | declarator_list ',' error
```

This declarator_list is found as part of a local or global declaration. The two cases can be distinguished by the nesting level contained in s_blknum once the Identifier has been processed by the symbol table manager: we should not find nesting level two, i.e., a parameter, or nesting level zero, i.e., an uninitialized symbol table entry, after the entry has been seen by the symbol table routine make_var().

```
int     g_offset = 1,           /* offset in global region */
        l_offset = 0,           /* offset in local region */
        l_max;                  /* size of local region */

all_var(symbol)
        register struct symtab * symbol;
{       extern struct symtab * make_var();
```

```
            symbol = make_var(symbol);

            /* if not in parameter region, assign suitable offset */
            switch (symbol->s_blknum) {
            default:                            /* local region */
                    symbol->s_offset = l_offset++;
            case 2:                             /* parameter region */
                    break;
            case 1:                             /* global region */
                    symbol->s_offset = g_offset++;
                    break;
            case 0:
                    bug("all_var");
            }
    }
```

For local variables, the offset is determined by the local offset counter l_offset; global variables are allocated through g_offset. Once the offset from the beginning of the appropriate activation record has been assigned to s_offset, the offset counter must be incremented by the size of the object just defined. We assume a word oriented machine, and we only deal with integer variables; we therefore always increment the offset counter by one.

Variables are defined in two contexts: global variables are scattered over the entire program, outside of functions, and local variables are found within each function.

Global allocation is the easier case: g_offset is initialized and then counted up throughout the compilation. Once the entire program has been recognized

```
    program
            :               { init(); }
              definitions
                            { all_program(); }
```

we find the size of the entire global activation record in g_offset:

```
    all_program()
    {
            blk_pop();

#ifdef  TRACE
            message("global region has %d word(s)", g_offset);
#endif
    }
```

We will use the first word in the global segment to return the result value of each function; therefore, g_offset is initialized as one and not zero.

For the local activation record we need to manage l_offset in a stack-fashion as we progress through the nested compound statements:

```
    compound_statement
            : '{'
                    { $<y_lab>$ = l_offset;
                      blk_push();
                    }
              declarations statements rr
```

```
{ if (l_offset > l_max)
        l_max = l_offset;
  l_offset = $<y_lab>2;
  blk_pop();
}
```

Notice that an embedded action may push a value on the *yacc* stack by assigning it to $$; the value is here later retrieved positionally as $2, just as if the action were a symbol. If we type the value stack, references to the stack element corresponding to the embedded action must be explicitly typed. The example shows that this is accomplished by placing the appropriate type information right into the stack reference.

The type in this case is a new one, namely a label. We therefore must add another component to the union describing the value stack:

```
%union  {
        struct symtab * y_sym;   /* Identifier */
        char * y_str;            /* Constant */
        int y_num;               /* count */
        int y_lab;               /* label */
        }
```

When processing of a compound_statement is started, l_offset designates the place in the local activation record where the first variable local to the compound_statement is to be allocated. For the outermost compound_statement, this is the initial value of l_offset, i.e., zero.

This starting offset is saved on the *yacc* value stack. Once the entire compound_statement has been taken care off, l_offset can be restored, and thus the area reserved for the compound_statement in the activation record can be reused.

Since we need to know the extent of the local activation record for a function, we need to monitor the high water mark for l_offset: the extent of the local activation record, l_max, is the maximum value which is reached by l_offset throughout all compound statements nested into the function. Before we start to process the outermost compound_statement for each function, we initialize l_max to zero:

```
function_definition
        : Identifier '('
                { make_func($1);
                  blk_push();
                }
          optional_parameter_list rp
          parameter_declarations
                { chk_parm($1, parm_default($4));
                  all_parm($4);
                  l_max = 0;
                }
          compound_statement
                { all_func($1); }
```

Once processing of a function is complete, l_max contains the required value:

```
all_func(symbol)
        struct symtab * symbol;
{
        blk_pop();

#ifdef  TRACE
        message("local region has %d word(s)", l_max);
#endif
}
```

Parameter offsets must be determined based on the position of the parameter within the `parameter_list` and on the declaration (if any!) of the parameter type. Therefore, we cannot assign the offsets immediately while processing the `parameter_list`. Instead, once all `parameter_declarations` have been taken care of and the remaining undeclared parameters have been defaulted, we can follow the chain linking the symbol table entries for the parameters and compute all offsets together:

```
all_parm(symbol)
        register struct symtab * symbol;
{       register int p_offset = 0;

        while (symbol)
        {       symbol->s_offset = p_offset ++;
                symbol = symbol->s_plist;
        }

#ifdef  TRACE
        message("parameter region has %d word(s)", p_offset);
#endif
}
```

The order in which the entries have been chained, as well as whether we increment `p_offset` from zero to positive offsets in a separate parameter segment, or decrement it from zero to negative offsets preceding the current local activation record, defines where we expect to find the argument values during execution.

In this implementation, we will push the argument values onto the stack in order from left to right. The address of the first argument pushed is recorded as the base address of the special parameter segment for each function. Parameter offsets are taken to be relative to this base address, and they must therefore increase from zero in the order of the `parameter_list` from left to right. We therefore must chain the parameters from left to right, and as we follow the chain, we will count `p_offset` up.

Unfortunately, thus far we have defined `parameter_list` using left recursion:

```
parameter_list
        : Identifier
                { $$ = link_parm($1, 0); }
        | parameter_list ',' Identifier
                { $$ = link_parm($3, $1);
                  yyerrok;
                }
        | error
                { $$ = 0; }
        | parameter_list error
```

```
        | parameter_list error Identifier
                { $$ = link_parm($3, $1);
                  yyerrok;
                }
        | parameter_list ',' error
```

This, however, implies that the list is *collected* from left to right, i.e., based on this rule the chain will run backwards!

The solution should be obvious: chaining happens as we reduce Identifier to parameter_list. We simply must assure that this happens from right to left, i.e., that we chain a new Identifier *before* an already existing parameter_list. This is precisely the case if we employ right recursion!

```
parameter_list
        : Identifier
                { $$ = link_parm($1, 0); }
        | Identifier ',' parameter_list
                { $$ = link_parm($1, $3);
                  yyerrok;
                }
        | error
                { $$ = 0; }
        | error parameter_list
                { $$ = $2; }
        | Identifier error parameter_list
                { $$ = link_parm($1, $3); }
        | error ',' parameter_list
                { $$ = $3;
                  yyerrok;
                }
```

Observe how easily the grammar can be modified in this fashion, without any adverse effects. Why can the same trick *not* be used to reverse the order of computation of the argument values?

The example from the previous chapter now illustrates what happens if the source program contains mistakes:

```
/*
 *      symtab demonstration, including errors
 */

main(a,b) int a,b;
{       a=b;
        {a;b;}
        if (a==b) {a;b;}
        if (a==b+1) a; else b;
        while (a==b) {a; break;}
        return;
}
int f() { int x; int y; return x+y; }
f(a,b)                  /* 14: duplicate function definition */
        int a;          /* undeclared parm b (not an error) */
{       int b,c;        /* 16: symbol b duplicates parm b */
        int c,d;        /* 17: duplicate symbol c */
        e=b;            /* 18: undeclared e */
```

```
            f=c+d;            /* 19: use func for var */
            a(b);            /* 20: use var for func */
            g();             /* 21: undefined function g */
        }
    h(a,a)                   /* 23: duplicate parameter */
            int f;           /* 24: not a parameter */
            int a;
            int a;           /* 26: duplicate parameter */
    { }
```

Output from the memory allocator:

```
    line 6 near "{": parameter region has 2 word(s)
    line 12 near "}": Popping b: variable, depth 2, offset 1
    line 12 near "}": Popping a: variable, depth 2, offset 0
    line 12 near "}": local region has 0 word(s)
    line 13 near "{": parameter region has 0 word(s)
    line 13 near "}": Popping y: variable, depth 3, offset 1
    line 13 near "}": Popping x: variable, depth 3, offset 0
    line 13 near "}": local region has 2 word(s)
    [error 1] line 14 near "(": duplicate function definition f
    [warning] line 16 near "{": function f should have 0 argument(s)
    line 16 near "{": parameter region has 2 word(s)
    [error 2] line 16 near "b": duplicate name b
    [error 3] line 17 near "c": duplicate name c
    [error 4] line 18 near ";": undeclared variable e
    [error 5] line 19 near ";": function f used as variable
    [error 6] line 20 near "(": variable a used as function
    line 22 near "}": Popping e: variable, depth 3, offset 0
    line 22 near "}": Popping d: variable, depth 3, offset 3
    line 22 near "}": Popping c: variable, depth 3, offset 2
    line 22 near "}": Popping c: variable, depth 3, offset 1
    line 22 near "}": Popping b: variable, depth 3, offset 0
    line 22 near "}": Popping b: variable, depth 2, offset 1
    line 22 near "}": Popping a: variable, depth 2, offset 0
    line 22 near "}": local region has 4 word(s)
    [error 7] line 23 near ")": duplicate parameter a
    [error 8] line 24 near "f": f is not a parameter
    [error 9] line 26 near "a": parameter a declared twice
    line 27 near "{": parameter region has 1 word(s)
    line 27 near "}": Popping f: variable, depth 2, offset 0
    line 27 near "}": Popping a: variable, depth 2, offset 0
    line 27 near "}": local region has 0 word(s)
    line 27: Popping h: function, depth 1, offset 0
    line 27: Popping f: function, depth 1, offset 0
    line 27: Popping main: function, depth 1, offset 0
    line 27: Popping g: undefined function, depth 1, offset 0
    [error 10] line 27: undefined function g
    line 27: global region has 1 word(s)
```

Note in particular that no offset is assigned to the undeclared variables, and that duplicate variable names cause some confusion in offset assignment. Basically, if the program contains errors, the resulting code is not guaranteed to be correct, but we must definitely take care that the compiler does not terminate in an unforeseen or unfriendly manner.

6.3 Problems

1. Suppose that the output from our compiler is to be processed by an assembler, i.e., the compiler will emit assembler code rather than machine code. What would be needed to allocate global variables by name? How would this simplify the compilation?

2. Suppose that *sampleC* is to be implemented on a machine in which one word occupies more than one addressable memory location (e.g., one word is made up of two separately-addressable bytes). What changes must be made to the memory allocation routines?

3. Many languages allow nesting of function definitions. What part of the allocation algorithm for *sampleC* would have to be changed so that function definitions could be nested? Keep in mind that a variable in an outer nesting block may be accessed as a global variable by an internally nested function (as long as there is no conflicting definition of its name in the internal function). How can the internal function reference such variables?

4. Using right recursion, it was simple to reverse the order of acceptance of the names in a `parameter_list`. What happens if we write an `argument_list` in a right recursive fashion? Since right recursion is not acceptable in this case, what other technique could be used to arrange for the arguments to a function call to be pushed onto the stack in reverse order?

Now that we are able to allocate memory in our fictitious machine, we are ready to produce a compiler that will generate code for it. Most of this chapter is devoted to showing how to generate code for a stack machine. Section 7.2 begins by defining the operations available on our machine, proceeds to the generation of code for the calculation of expression values and for assignment statements, and then considers the problems of generating code to implement if and while control structures. Very little attempt is made to optimize the generated code; however, the problems at the end of the chapter suggest how some additional efficiency could be achieved.

7.1 Principles

The code generation policy determines what instructions need to be issued for each action that can be expressed in the programming language. A straightforward approach, given a stack machine, is to arrange for the expressions to be converted to postfix notation. Making local and global variables addressable might pose a problem, depending on the addressing structure of the target machine.

The only difficult aspect, which for an actual implementation is quite important, is the design of the calling sequence for function calls. For our example we will assume "suitable" instructions; managing the activation record stack on a real machine may require that appropriate subprograms be designed and linked with each compiled program. Such subprograms are a natural place to insert traces for debugging or profiling of the compiled code.

The implementation of iteration and decision statements usually requires a number of forward branches, e.g., around the else part of an if statement. Unfortunately, these forward branch instructions usually have to be emitted twice: once with an unknown target address, so that space for the instruction is reserved, and later with the corrected address. If we actually construct a program in memory, we need to fix the relevant memory locations.

If we decide to emit assembler text, we could use an origin pseudo-instruction to direct the assembler later to the proper program address so that we may reissue the jump instruction once we know its actual target address. A much better technique in this case, however, is to simply generate a symbolic label, and let the assembler deal with the forward branch.

The break and continue statements of *sampleC* require stacks onto which the relevant label information is pushed when a while or similar statement is processed. If a switch statement is included in the language, two stacks are required, since then the information for continue can significantly differ from the information for break. The stacks also serve to determine the legality of the use of these statements, a semantic test which we had deliberately postponed in chapter 5.

7.2 Example

We will demonstrate how to generate assembler code for our fictitious machine. The assembler source format is similar to that of many existing assemblers: one instruction per line; an optional label field starts in column one; the second, mandatory field contains a mnemonic operation code; a third field might contain an operation modifier or other information; fields are separated by white space; and a comment may follow at the end of the line. The details of the format are not really important at this point, since they are easily changed in the code generation routines.

As a quick overview of the available instructions, consider their definition in the following header file *gen.h*:

```
/*
 *      operation codes for pseudo machine
 */

#define OP_ALU    "alu"         /* arithmetic-logic-op  */
#define OP_DEC    "dec"         /* region,offset        */
#define OP_INC    "inc"         /* region,offset        */
#define OP_LOAD   "load"        /* region,offset        */
#define OP_STORE  "store"       /* region,offset        */
#define OP_POP    "pop"         /*                      */
#define OP_JUMPZ  "jumpz"       /* label                */
#define OP_JUMP   "jump"        /* label                */
#define OP_CALL   "call"        /* parm-count,address   */
#define OP_ENTRY  "entry"       /* local-frame-size     */
#define OP_RETURN "return"      /*                      */

/*
 *      region modifiers
 */

#define MOD_GLOBAL "gbl"        /* global region        */
#define MOD_PARAM  "par"        /* parameter region     */
#define MOD_LOCAL  "lcl"        /* local region         */
#define MOD_IMMED  "con"        /* load only: Constant   */

/*
 *      OP_ALU modifiers
 */

#define ALU_ADD "+"             /* addition             */
#define ALU_SUB "-"             /* subtraction          */
#define ALU_MUL "*"             /* multiplication       */
#define ALU_DIV "/"             /* division             */
#define ALU_MOD "%"             /* remainder            */
#define ALU_LT  "<"             /* compares as: <       */
#define ALU_GT  ">"             /*              >        */
#define ALU_LE  "<="            /*              <=       */
#define ALU_GE  ">="            /*              >=       */
#define ALU_EQ  "=="            /*              ==       */
#define ALU_NE  "!="            /*              !=       */
#define ALU_AND "&"             /* bit-wise and         */
#define ALU_OR  "|"             /* bit-wise or          */
#define ALU_XOR "^"             /* bit-wise excl. or    */
```

```
/*
 *      typed functions, code generator
 */

char * gen_mod();                    /* region modifier */
```

The precise definition of each instruction is implied by the simulator presented in chapter 8. For the purposes of code generation, the following remarks should suffice to characterize the effect of each instruction:

Our fictitious machine is a stack machine. Code generation for expressions is therefore quite simple: the values of variables and constants must be pushed onto the stack, using load instructions provided for this purpose, and for operators an alu instruction must be issued. The alu instruction has a modifier which indicates what arithmetic or logic operation is to be performed on the two elements on top of the stack. The result of the operation then replaces the two elements on the stack. Modifiers happen to exist corresponding to each operator in *sampleC*.

Assignments, of course, correspond to store instructions. In *sampleC*, however, assignment can be an embedded operation. The store instruction therefore will *not* remove a value from the stack. This is instead accomplished by an explicit pop instruction, which must be coded whenever an expression value is to be discarded.

Code generation for if and while statements involves the construction of appropriate branching instructions. There are some forward references, e.g., to the else part of an if statement; these are handled by generating unique labels based on a counter, passing them on the semantic stack in *yacc* actions, and letting the assembler resolve the definitions.

break and continue pose a more subtle problem: in *sampleC* they are allowed only inside a while loop. This is best monitored by separate stacks, on which each while statement is expected to deposit appropriate labels, which are removed at the end of the dependent statement.

Function calls are handled by a call instruction, which expects the function arguments to be on the stack. This instruction contains the number of actual arguments, so that the parameter segment can be set up properly.

At the beginning of a function we need to code an entry instruction specifying the amount of space to reserve on the stack for local variables. The combination of call and entry instructions is assumed to handle all problems associated with parameter passing and dynamic allocation of local variables.

The return instruction will remove the local activation record from the stack, and restore all relevant hardware registers. If the return instruction is preceded by the evaluation of an expression, the value must be saved prior to return, since code following call must be generated to remove all arguments from the stack. This code is also expected to push any result value of a function back onto the stack.

We will again show additions to the grammar next to the new code generation functions called by these actions. A complete listing is in section 6 in the appendix. Let us start by considering code generation for arithmetic expressions:

```
        binary
                : binary '+' binary
                        { gen_alu(ALU_ADD, "+"); }
```

Like almost all code generation functions, gen_alu() merely consists of a printf() library function call:

```
gen_alu(mod, comment)
        char * mod;              /* mnemonic modifier */
        char * comment;         /* instruction comment */
{
        printf("\t%s\t%s\t\t; %s\n", OP_ALU, mod, comment);
}
```

alu is the class of arithmetic operations; each operation pops two values off the stack, combines them, and pushes the result back on the stack. For this to work, the operands of each arithmetic operation must be on the stack. Initially, we must therefore push constants and the values of variables as we encounter them in an expression:

```
        binary
                : Constant
                        { gen_li($1); }
```

s_lookup() dynamically saved the text of a Constant and pushed a pointer to this text onto the *yacc* stack. We can now use this text to produce a load immediate instruction; in this fashion the lexical analyzer defines the entire representation of a Constant.

```
gen_li(const)
        char * const;           /* Constant value */
{
        printf("\t%s\t%s,%s\n", OP_LOAD, MOD_IMMED, const);
}
```

In order to load the value of a variable, we must consult the symbol table:

```
%{
#define OFFSET(x)       ( ((struct symtab *) x) -> s_offset )
#define NAME(x)         ( ((struct symtab *) x) -> s_name )
%}
%%

        binary
                : Identifier
                        { chk_var($1);
                          gen(OP_LOAD, gen_mod($1), OFFSET($1), NAME($1));
                        }
```

gen_mod() constructs an appropriate area modifier from s_blknum, OFFSET() and NAME() retrieve the relevant fields from the symbol table entry, and gen() composes the various fields into an instruction:

```
        char * gen_mod(symbol)
                struct symtab * symbol;
        {
                switch (symbol->s_blknum) {
```

```
                case 1:
                        return MOD_GLOBAL;
                case 2:
                        return MOD_PARAM;
                }
                return MOD_LOCAL;
        }

        gen(op, mod, val, comment)
                char * op;                    /* mnemonic operation code */
                char * mod;                   /* mnemonic modifier */
                int val;                      /* offset field */
                char * comment;               /* instruction comment */
        {
                printf("\t%s\t%s,%d\t\t; %s\n", op, mod, val, comment);
        }
```

For assignments, we must generate code to evaluate the value to be assigned. A simple assignment then is accomplished with a store instruction; for composite assignments, load must precede and the appropriate alu instruction must follow the code generated for the right hand side, before the store instruction can be issued. store does *not* pop the stored value off the stack, so that embedded assignments work.

```
        binary
                : Identifier '=' binary
                        { chk_var($1);
                          gen(OP_STORE, gen_mod($1), OFFSET($1), NAME($1));
                        }
                | Identifier PE
                        { chk_var($1);
                          gen(OP_LOAD, gen_mod($1), OFFSET($1), NAME($1));
                        }
                  binary
                        { gen_alu(ALU_ADD, "+");
                          gen(OP_STORE, gen_mod($1), OFFSET($1), NAME($1));
                        }
```

We are "fortunate" to have specific machine instructions for increment and decrement operations, which modify memory and additionally deposit their result on the stack. As an example, here is the increment operation:

```
        binary
                : PP Identifier
                        { chk_var($2);
                          gen(OP_INC, gen_mod($2), OFFSET($2), NAME($2));
                        }
```

The comma operator in C causes sequential evaluation of two expressions: the left operand is evaluated and discarded, then the right operand is evaluated and delivers the result. Discarding a value means popping the stack:

```
        expression
                : binary
                | expression ','
                        { gen_pr(OP_POP, "discard"); }
                  binary
```

```
                           { yyerrok; }
```

The pop instruction does just that. As a result of reducing the second binary, code will be generated to leave another result on the stack. gen_pr() will later also be used to generate return instructions.

```
        gen_pr(op, comment)
                char * op;              /* mnemonic operation code */
                char * comment;         /* instruction comment */
        {
                printf("\t%s\t\t\t; %s\n", op, comment);
        }
```

We are now ready to consider some statements. Nothing needs to be generated for an empty statement. A compound_statement is handled automatically as the sequence of its constituents. The evaluation of an expression as a statement resembles the use of a comma operator: the resulting expression value must be discarded.

```
        statement
                : sc
                | compound_statement
                | expression sc
                        { gen_pr(OP_POP, "clear stack"); }
```

Control structures are implemented through branching instructions. The easiest case is the if statement:

```
        %type    <y_lab> if_prefix
        %%
        if_prefix
                : IF '(' expression rp
                        { $$ = gen_jump(OP_JUMPZ, new_label(), "IF"); }
```

Code for the expression is generated as usual, leaving a value behind on the stack. The jumpz instruction will effect a branch if this value is zero; it will remove the value from the stack in either case.

```
        int gen_jump(op, label, comment)
                char * op;              /* mnemonic operation code */
                int label;              /* target of jump */
                char * comment;         /* instruction comment */
        {
                printf("\t%s\t%s\t\t; %s\n", op, format_label(label),
                        comment);
                return label;
        }
```

new_label() is a function, which for each call must return a new, unique label. We create unique labels by counting up a static integer variable; the resulting value can be passed along on the *yacc* stack (gen_jump() returns the label value for this purpose). A single function format_label() is used to represent the unique integer values as labels acceptable to an assembler in various contexts.

```
        int new_label()
        {       static int next_label = 0;
```

```
                return ++next_label;
        }

        #define LABEL    "$$%d"

        static char * format_label(label)
                int label;
        {       static char buffer[sizeof LABEL + 2];

                sprintf(buffer, LABEL, label);
                return buffer;
        }
```

if_prefix took care of evaluating the condition and implementing the decision by means of a branch to an — as yet undefined — label, which if_prefix deposited on the *yacc* stack. The branch is designed to bypass the then part of the if statement if the condition is not met. We must define the label following the dependent statement:

```
        statement
                : if_prefix statement
                        { gen_label($1); }
```

gen_label() arranges for a label definition using an equ pseudo-operation:

```
        int gen_label(label)
                int label;
        {
                printf("%s\tequ\t*\n", format_label(label));
                return label;
        }
```

If there is an else part, we must define the label at the beginning of the else part. It must, however, be preceded by an unconditional branch which transfers control from the end of the then part directly to the end of the if statement. Once again we use the *yacc* stack to pass the undefined labels forward to the point where they can be defined:

```
        statement
                : if_prefix statement ELSE
                        { $<y_lab>$ = gen_jump(OP_JUMP, new_label(),
                                "past ELSE");
                          gen_label($1);
                        }
                  statement
                        { gen_label($<y_lab>4); }
```

Input errors can invalidate the generated code. We must generate a branching instruction in the following case:

```
        if_prefix
                : IF error
                        { $$ = gen_jump(OP_JUMPZ, new_label(), "IF"); }
```

If there is no suitable value on the stack, jumpz will cause an underflow. If we do not generate a branch, but only return a value obtained from new_label(), we might cause a stack overflow in the long run!

The while loop is handled using the same techniques:

```
%type    <y_lab> loop_prefix
%%

loop_prefix
        : WHILE '('
                { $<y_lab>$ = gen_label(new_label());
                  push_continue($<y_lab>$);
                }
            expression rp
                { $$ = $<y_lab>3; }
        | WHILE error
                { $$ = gen_label(new_label());
                  push_continue($$);
                }
```

The `loop_prefix` first defines a new label marking the continuation point. Then code for the condition is generated. The label is passed as a result.

The branch instruction to a second, undefined label, testing the condition value, is generated at the statement level. In this fashion, it can be passed in a second slot on the *yacc* stack:

```
statement
        : loop_prefix
                { $<y_lab>$ = gen_jump(OP_JUMPZ, new_label(),
                    "WHILE");
                  push_break($<y_lab>$);
                }
            statement
                { gen_jump(OP_JUMP, $1, "repeat WHILE");
                  gen_label($<y_lab>2);
                  pop_break();
                  pop_continue();
                }
```

Code for the dependent statement can then be generated. An unconditional branch to the continuation point follows, and then the label must be defined to which we branch when we want to leave the while construct.

The resulting code is not optimally efficient: if we moved the code for the condition to *follow* the dependent statement, we could use the conditional branch to iterate the loop and thus save one branch per iteration. This, however, would require that we save the code for an expression somewhere.

sampleC has break and continue statements, which within a while construct transfer control to the termination or iteration points. The statements must be implemented as unconditional jumps, and we must supply appropriate labels. Since while statements can be nested, the labels must be stacked; since in C a switch establishes a new nesting level for break but not for continue, we chose to implement two stacks, although *sampleC* could be implemented with one.

We have already pushed the stacks in the `loop_prefix` and in the while statement expansion; following the while construct, we have popped the labels. Assuming the existence of push() and pop() stack management functions, the routines can be defined as follows:

```
        push_break(label)
                int label;
        {
                b_top = push(b_top, label);
        }

        push_continue(label)
                int label;
        {
                c_top = push(c_top, label);
        }

        pop_break()
        {
                b_top = pop(b_top);
        }

        pop_continue()
        {
                c_top = pop(c_top);
        }
```

Assuming a function top() to inspect a stack, break and continue are simple to implement:

```
        statement
                : BREAK sc
                        { gen_break(); }
                | CONTINUE sc
                        { gen_continue(); }

        gen_break()
        {
                gen_jump(OP_JUMP, top(b_top), "BREAK");
        }

        gen_continue()
        {
                gen_jump(OP_JUMP, top(c_top), "CONTINUE");
        }
```

The stack management itself is not particularly difficult. We define a structure to hold an internal label and to be linked as a stack:

```
        static struct bc_stack {
                int bc_label;               /* label from new_label */
                struct bc_stack * bc_next;
                } * b_top,                  /* head of break stack */
                  * c_top;                  /* head of continue stack */
```

b_top is a pointer to the top element on the break stack. c_top similarly points to the continue stack. Both pointers are null if the stacks are empty, i.e., if break and continue statements are not permitted.

push() is given a pointer to a stack and a label value to push. It returns a pointer to the new element, to which the rest of the stack has been linked. The result must be assigned to the pointer passed as an argument in order to complete the push operation.

```
static struct bc_stack * push(stack, label)
        struct bc_stack * stack;
        int label;
{       struct bc_stack * new_entry = (struct bc_stack *)
                calloc(1, sizeof(struct bc_stack));

        if (new_entry)
        {       new_entry->bc_next = stack;
                new_entry->bc_label = label;
                return new_entry;
        }
        fatal("No more room to compile loops.");
        /*NOTREACHED*/
}
```

Similarly, pop() discards the top element of a stack and returns a pointer to the rest, which also must be assigned to the stack pointer passed as an argument.

```
static struct bc_stack * pop(stack)
        struct bc_stack * stack;
{       struct bc_stack * old_entry;

        if (stack)
        {       old_entry = stack;
                stack = old_entry->bc_next;
                cfree(old_entry);
                return stack;
        }
        bug("break/continue stack underflow");
        /*NOTREACHED*/
}
```

In top() semantic testing of the legitimacy of break or continue calls takes place:

```
static int top(stack)
        struct bc_stack * stack;
{
        if (! stack)
        {       error("no loop open");
                return 0;
        }
        else
                return stack->bc_label;
}
```

Only one operation remains to be implemented: we need to generate code for a function call, for initializing the activation record of a new function, and for returning from the function call. The call instruction is used to pass control to a function:

```
binary
        : Identifier '('
                { chk_func($1); }
```

```
            optional_argument_list rp
                    { gen_call($1,$4); }
```

Since the argument expressions are reduced first, the function will find the parameter values on the stack. Upon return from the function, we must therefore pop all these values off the stack. There is no easy way to pass the result on the stack. We therefore decided to pass the result at the very beginning of the global segment; gen_call() must push this value onto the stack, where the function value is really expected to replace the arguments following the call:

```
    gen_call(symbol, count)
            struct symtab * symbol; /* function */
            int count;              /* # of arguments */
    {
            chk_parm(symbol, count);
            printf("\t%s\t%d,%s\n", OP_CALL, count, symbol->s_name);
            while (count-- > 0)
                    gen_pr(OP_POP, "pop argument");
            gen(OP_LOAD, MOD_GLOBAL, 0, "push result");
    }
```

There is a return instruction which takes care of returning control to the point following the call instruction. call will push the return address, return will remove it; the instructions may therefore be used recursively. If a value is to be returned, it will be found on the stack, and it has to be moved to the result word at the beginning of the global segment before we can issue the return instruction:

```
    statement
        : RETURN sc
                { gen_pr(OP_RETURN, "RETURN"); }
        | RETURN expression sc
                { gen(OP_STORE, MOD_GLOBAL, 0, "save result");
                  gen_pr(OP_RETURN, "RETURN");
                }
```

call pushes the return address onto the stack. When a function is called, it must push the address of the old activation record onto the stack, it must set the register marking the beginning of the new, current activation record to the top of the stack, and the register marking the top of the stack must be changed to accommodate the new activation record. All this is taken care of by the entry instruction, which expects the size of the new activation record as a parameter:

```
    function_definition
            : Identifier '('
                    { make_func($1);
                      blk_push();
                    }
            optional_parameter_list rp
            parameter_declarations
                    { chk_parm($1, parm_default($4));
                      all_parm($4);
                      l_max = 0;
                      $<y_lab>$ = gen_entry($1);
                    }
            compound_statement
```

```
                        { all_func($1);
                          gen_pr(OP_RETURN, "end of function");
                          fix_entry($1, $<y_lab>7);
                        }
```

Unfortunately, we do not know the size of the activation record when we begin to compile the function. We therefore emit a new label as parameter of the entry instruction and pass it on the *yacc* stack:

```
        int gen_entry(symbol)
                struct symtab * symbol; /* function */
        {       int label = new_label();

                printf("%s\t", symbol->s_name);
                printf("%s\t%s\n", OP_ENTRY, format_label(label));
                return label;
        }
```

Following compilation of the function body we can define this label as required:

```
        fix_entry(symbol, label)
                struct symtab * symbol; /* function */
                int label;
        {       extern int l_max;       /* size of local region */

                printf("%s\tequ\t%d\t\t; %s\n", format_label(label),
                        l_max, symbol->s_name);
        }
```

We are through: when we complete compilation of the entire program, we know the size of the global segment, and we have required that execution start with a call to the main() function, which must be somewhere in the program. This information is passed on through an end pseudo-operation:

```
        program
                :               { init(); }
                  definitions
                                { end_program(); }


        end_program()
        {       extern int g_offset;    /* size of global region */

                all_program();          /* allocate global variables */
                printf("\tend\t%d,main\n", g_offset);
        }
```

As an example of code generation, consider the following implementation of Euclid's algorithm to compute the greatest common divisor of two positive integers:

```
/*
 *      Euclid's algorithm
 */

main()
{       int a,b;

        a = 36;
        b = 54;

        while (a != b)
               if (a > b)
                      a -= b;
               else
                      b -= a;
}
```

The resulting assembler code is as follows:

```
main    entry   $$1
        load    con,36
        store   lcl,0           ; a
        pop                     ; clear stack
        load    con,54
        store   lcl,1           ; b
        pop                     ; clear stack
$$2     equ     *
        load    lcl,0           ; a
        load    lcl,1           ; b
        alu     !=              ; !=
        jumpz   $$3             ; WHILE
        load    lcl,0           ; a
        load    lcl,1           ; b
        alu     >               ; >
        jumpz   $$4             ; IF
        load    lcl,0           ; a
        load    lcl,1           ; b
        alu     -               ; -
        store   lcl,0           ; a
        pop                     ; clear stack
        jump    $$5             ; past ELSE
$$4     equ     *
        load    lcl,1           ; b
        load    lcl,0           ; a
        alu     -               ; -
        store   lcl,1           ; b
        pop                     ; clear stack
$$5     equ     *
        jump    $$2             ; repeat WHILE
$$3     equ     *
        return                  ; end of function
$$1     equ     2               ; main
        end     1,main
```

7.3 Problems

1. Implement *sampleC* on a real machine. One approach is to specify the instructions used in this chapter as macros on the real machine. Another approach is to modify the code generator directly, still based on the assumption of a stack machine. An implementation which makes best use of a different architecture, e.g., of a register machine, is significantly harder to code.

2. The Euclid's algorithm example shows that the generated assembler code is not always terribly efficient. For example, part of the code generated is:

```
        jump    $$5                 ; past ELSE
        . . .
$$5     equ     *
        jump    $$2                 ; repeat WHILE
```

Non-sequential transfers of control can only be made to points marked with a label. If the definition of such a label directly precedes a jump, the code can be optimized by equating the label to the target of the jump. In this example, that would generate:

```
$$5         equ     $$2
```

instead of the equ above. How can this be accomplished? Hint: one method would involve a postprocessor, a program which would examine the output of the compiler and optimize it before passing it to the assembler. Can the optimization be done within the one-pass compiler itself?

3. Another inefficiency involves the problem of unreachable code. E.g., when a return statement precedes the end of a function, our *sampleC* compiler will generate two return instructions in a row. In fact, this will usually happen for a function which returns a value. How can this extra return instruction be eliminated?

4. Still another inefficiency involves consecutive load pop sequences. E.g., when a statement consists of a function call (with the function result ignored), our compiler will load the result value following the call, only to immediately pop it again in concluding the statement. How can this useless sequence be eliminated?

The preceding chapter demonstrated that it is relatively simple to construct a code generator if the target machine architecture is close enough to the source language. Once the *implementation*, i.e., a memory allocation policy and code sequences for the various actions in the source language, has been defined, we can turn to simulation of a suitable machine architecture as one means of completing the programming system. This chapter will show the construction of a simulator for the machine assumed in the previous two chapters, and it will show how a load-and-go system is developed using such a simulator. The discussion is necessarily quite specific to *sampleC*. However, several languages have been implemented in a similar fashion, e.g., Pascal and Modula-2.

8.1 A machine simulator

A simulator for our fictitious machine is actually quite simple to construct. First we need to define numerical codes for the individual instructions and instruction modifiers. The resulting header file *sim.h* provides a different representation for all names previously defined in *gen.h*:

```
/*
 *      operation codes for pseudo machine
 */

#define OP_ALU    1       /* alu   arithmetic-logic-op   */
#define OP_DEC    2       /* dec   region,offset         */
#define OP_INC    3       /* inc   region,offset         */
#define OP_LOAD   4       /* load  region,offset         */
#define OP_STORE  5       /* store region,offset         */
#define OP_POP    6       /* pop                         */
#define OP_JUMPZ  7       /* jumpz label                 */
#define OP_JUMP   8       /* jump  label                 */
#define OP_CALL   9       /* call  routine-address       */
#define OP_ENTRY  10      /* entry local-frame-size      */
#define OP_RETURN 11      /* return                      */

/*
 *      region modifiers
 */

#define MOD_GLOBAL 1      /* global region      */
#define MOD_PARAM  2      /* parameter region   */
#define MOD_LOCAL  3      /* local region       */
#define MOD_IMMED  4      /* load only: Constant */

/*
 *      OP_ALU modifiers
 */

#define ALU_ADD 1         /* addition     */
#define ALU_SUB 2         /* subtraction  */
```

```
#define ALU_MUL 3          /* multiplication          */
#define ALU_DIV 4          /* division                */
#define ALU_MOD 5          /* remainder               */
#define ALU_LT  6          /* compares as: <          */
#define ALU_GT  7          /*              >          */
#define ALU_LE  8          /*              <=         */
#define ALU_GE  9          /*              >=         */
#define ALU_EQ  10         /*              ==         */
#define ALU_NE  11         /*              !=         */
#define ALU_AND 12         /* bit-wise and            */
#define ALU_OR  13         /* bit-wise or             */
#define ALU_XOR 14         /* bit-wise excl. or       */
```

We start by defining arrays for program and data space of our fictitious machine.
Data cells are represented as integers, but for program cells we choose a structure to
simplify decoding:

```
struct prog {
        short p_op;        /* operation code */
        short p_mod;       /* modifier */
        int p_val;         /* offset or other value */
        };


/*
 *      tunable limits
 */

#define L_PROG  200        /* max. program size */
#define L_DATA  100        /* max. area for stack, etc. */
#define DIM(x)  (sizeof x / sizeof x[0]) /* extent */
```

At least the maximum size of the program segment and the prog structure must be
added to the header file; we will need them once we generate code. Now for the
arrays:

```
#include "sim.h"

/*
 *      data and program memory
 */

static int data[L_DATA];
extern struct prog prog[];
```

We will define prog[] in the code generation module. This way we can check dimen-
sional extents using the macro DIM() shown above, and we do not depend on the constant used for dimensioning the vector.

Next we define the registers. There is an internal register inst which holds the
current instruction to simplify decoding. Various positions in the data segment are
marked by the registers G, P, L, and T. G marks the beginning of the global segment;
this is the constant index zero. P marks the beginning of the current parameter segment preceding the activation record. L marks the beginning of the current local segment, i.e., the activation record. T marks the top of the stack, i.e., the first available
word following the local segment and all values currently pushed onto the stack.

```
/*
 *      registers
 */

static struct prog * inst;      /* -> current instruction */
#define G          0            /* global segment */
static int P;                   /* current parameter segment */
static int L;                   /* current local segment */
static int T;                   /* top of stack */
```

Certain abbreviations turn out to be convenient: TOP and NEXT refer to the top-most two values on the stack; PUSH can be assigned to and causes a value to be pushed onto the stack; POP is an operation which will discard the top element on the stack; RESULT refers to the word at the beginning of the data segment, which we use in returning a result value from a function; and MEMORY is a short-hand notation for the memory cell addressed by the current instruction.

```
/*
 *      shorthand notations
 */

#define TOP      data[T-1]       /* right operand: top of stack */
#define NEXT     data[T-2]       /* left operand: below TOP */
#define PUSH     data[T++]       /* new cell to come onto stack */
#define POP      -- T            /* -> discarded cell from stack */
#define MEMORY   data[address()] /* effectively addressed cell */
#define RESULT   data[G]         /* result value of function */
```

These definitions effectively extend the language in which the simulator is written. Here they serve to improve the self-documentation of the code; excessive use of such language extensions, however, tends to obscure the resulting program and make it harder to modify.

MEMORY employs the function address() to determine which cell in data[] the current instruction references:

```
static int address()    /* effective current data address */
{       register int ad;
        switch (inst->p_mod) {
        case MOD_GLOBAL:
                ad = G;
                break;
        case MOD_PARAM:
                ad = P;
                break;
        case MOD_LOCAL:
                ad = L;
                break;
        default:
                bug("invalid p_mod");
        }
        ad += inst->p_val;
        if (ad < 0 || ad >= T)
                bug("invalid effective address");
        return ad;
}
```

The effective address results from adding an offset in the instruction to the base address of the segment indicated by the instruction modifier. This address must be within the current extent of the data segment.

We are ready to design the basic execution cycle of our simulator. simulate() obtains its information from the end statement of the compiled program: when this pseudo-instruction is generated, we know pc_limit, the size of the compiled program; global, the size of the global segment; and pc, the position in the program segment at which simulation should commence, i.e., the address of the main() function in the compiled program. These values can be passed to simulate(); pc additionally will serve as the program counter of the simulated machine:

```
simulate(pc_limit, global, pc)
        int pc_limit, global, pc;
{
        /* initialize */

        printf("\nExecution begins...\n\n");

        for (;;)
        {       /* fetch */
                if (pc < 0 || pc >= pc_limit)
                        bug("pc not in program area");
                inst = &prog[pc++];

                /* decode operation and dispatch */
                switch (inst->p_op) {
                default:
                        printf("%d:\thalt\n", inst-prog);
                        return;

                /* other instructions */
                }
        }
}
```

For the moment, we shall defer initialization of the P, L, and T registers. This can be designed once we have implemented the function calling sequence: we must initialize the registers and the stack in such a way that a return from main() will halt the machine.

Let us consider the various instructions in the order in which they were introduced in chapter 7.

alu is simple: we dispatch the instruction modifier with another switch and thus map the modifier to the appropriate C operator. In order to keep the example simple, we do not guard against arithmetic exceptions such as, e.g., division by zero. We do, however, attempt to check that operands are in fact available on the stack; they are definitely not if there is not enough room for two operands between the beginning of the local segment (in L) and the top of the stack (in T). We just show a few typical examples:

```
case OP_ALU:
        if (T <= L+1)
                bug("simulator stack underflow");
        switch (inst->p_mod) {
        default:
                bug("illegal ALU instruction");
        case ALU_ADD:
                NEXT += TOP;
                break;
        case ALU_LT:
                NEXT = NEXT < TOP;
                break;
        }
        POP;
        break;
```

If the compilation encountered no errors, stack underflow really is a bug, i.e., a problem which should not happen; if the program contained errors, the stack may underflow as a consequence of unavoidable faulty code generation. Since our test for stack underflow cannot be very restrictive anyhow, we do consider the situation to be a bug.

For load we must distinguish between loading the value of a variable from MEMORY and loading the value of a Constant directly from the instruction. We monitor that the stack does not overflow if we push a new value.

```
case OP_LOAD:
        if (T >= DIM(data))
                fatal("Too much data.");
        if (inst->p_mod == MOD_IMMED)
                PUSH = inst->p_val;
        else
                PUSH = MEMORY;
        break;
```

store copies a value from the stack to memory. We attempt to check that there actually is a value on the stack.

```
case OP_STORE:
        if (T <= L)
                bug("simulator stack underflow");
        printf("%d:\tstore\t%d,%d\tto %d\n",
                inst-prog, inst->p_mod,
                inst->p_val, MEMORY = TOP);
        break;
```

store is a good place to show the effects of simulation: we trace the instruction and show the value stored.

inc and dec are responsible not only for modifying memory, but also for pushing the result onto the stack, which should not overflow:

```
case OP_INC:
        if (T >= DIM(data))
                fatal("Too much data.");
        printf("%d:\tinc\t%d,%d\tto %d\n",
                inst-prog, inst->p_mod,
```

```
                                inst->p_val, PUSH = ++ MEMORY);
                        break;

                case OP_DEC:
                        if (T >= DIM(data))
                                fatal("Too much data.");
                        printf("%d:\tdec\t%d,%d\tto %d\n",
                                inst-prog, inst->p_mod,
                                inst->p_val, PUSH = -- MEMORY);
                        break;
```

Both instructions are traced, so that all modifications of memory can be followed.

pop will discard an element from the stack, as long as it seems plausible that one exists:

```
                case OP_POP:
                        if (T <= L)
                                bug("simulator stack underflow");
                        POP;
                        break;
```

jump makes an assignment to the program counter pc. Once the simulation loop continues, the new value will be used as the address of the next instruction. The address is verified during instruction fetch.

```
                case OP_JUMP:
                        printf("%d:\tjump\t%d\n", inst-prog,
                                inst->p_val);
                        pc = inst->p_val;
                        break;
```

jumpz pops a value off the stack and tests it. If the value is zero, an assignment to the program counter is made so that the jump takes place:

```
                case OP_JUMPZ:
                        if (T <= L)
                                bug("simulator stack underflow");
                        if (data[POP] == 0)
                        {       printf("%d:\tjumpz\t%d\n",
                                        inst-prog, inst->p_val);
                                pc = inst->p_val;
                        }
                        break;
```

If a jump takes place, we trace the instruction, so that the flow of execution can be followed.

call pushes the program counter onto the stack. Since during instruction fetch the program counter is set to point to the next instruction, this will be the proper return address. call also pushes the address of the current parameter segment onto the stack, and sets register P to point to the new parameter segment on the stack; since the number of arguments to be passed is stored in the instruction modifier of call, and since the arguments have been pushed onto the stack prior to call, the new value of P is easily computed. A jump then takes place to the desired function. call is traced, too:

```
case OP_CALL:
        printf("%d:\tcall\t%d\n", inst-prog,
                inst->p_val);
        PUSH = pc;
        pc = inst->p_val;
        PUSH = P;
        P = T - 2 - inst->p_mod;
        break;
```

Once the new function is entered, the address of the old local segment (in L) must be pushed onto the stack. The new local segment is established on top of the stack by setting L to the current top of the stack (in T) and incrementing T by the size of the new local segment. All of this is the job of the entry instruction:

```
case OP_ENTRY:
        PUSH = L;
        L = T;
        T += inst->p_val;
        if (T >= DIM(data))
                fatal("Too much data.");
        break;
```

Upon return, we must pop the current local segment by setting T to its starting address (in L). The addresses of the previous local segment and of the previous parameter segment can then be found on the stack. Just below we find the return address. All three words must also be popped from the stack:

```
case OP_RETURN:
        if (T < L)
                bug("simulator stack underflow");
        T = L;
        L = data[POP];
        P = data[POP];
        pc = data[POP];
        printf("%d:\treturn\t%d to %d\n",
                inst-prog, RESULT, pc);
        break;
```

A function result, if any, will later be pushed from RESULT; we can show it in the trace of the return instruction just in case.

Function calling and return could still be simplified: we do not really need to generate pop instructions to dispose of the parameter segment; the original stack top could be restored as the beginning of the current parameter segment. Additionally, the RESULT word is not necessary: since the original stack top can be determined, return can always move a result value there. While this shortens the generated code, it adds complexity to the simulator; the entire approach is not very realistic in either case — return hardware instructions tend to be much simpler!

This completes the simulator. All that remains is the initialization. We just saw that return expects a program counter and a parameter segment address deposited by call and a local segment address deposited by entry on top of the stack. We need to simulate a call to main(); once we return, the simulator should halt.

Halting is accomplished by placing a zero operation code into the first location in program memory. This will cause all undefined jumps or calls to halt the simulator, since they would transfer control to location zero. Additionally we place zero as return address on the stack, before we start interpretation with the entry instruction in main(); thus, the return from main() will also halt the simulation. Initial values for P and L are not required, since these values will not be used. We also may leave the value of P pushed by the simulated call on the stack uninitialized:

```
if (global >= DIM(data))
        fatal("Not enough room for global data.");
T = global + 2;
```

Program memory is static and as such initialized to zero.

8.2 In-core code generation

Once we turn to simulation, an attractive approach is to let the compiler generate code directly in the simulated memory. After a program has been — successfully — compiled, it can be immediately "executed."

In-core code generation is identical to emitting assembler text as far as the generated instruction sequences are concerned. Forward references can, however, no longer be passed on to a two-pass assembler for resolution; they must be fixed up by the compiler, before simulation can begin. Depending on instruction format, a significant amount of bit manipulation may be required to emit code; this is the primary area where generating assembler text avoids a lot of trouble and enhances portability of the compiler.

In this section we will exhibit in-core code generation utilities for *sampleC* to be used in conjunction with the simulator presented in the previous section. It turns out that the new functions are identical in name and calling sequence to the code generation functions constructed in chapter 7. A new header file, *sim.h*, provides different representations for the operation codes, but otherwise the parser can remain entirely unchanged!

We start by defining program memory and a routine to add an instruction to it. Just like an assembler, the code generator needs a private program counter pc which points to the next available program memory location. Eventually, pc will be passed to the simulator as pc_limit, since it defines the used size of the program segment once code generation is complete.

```
#include "sim.h"
#include "symtab.h"

/*
 *      program memory
 */
struct prog prog[L_PROG];
static int pc = 1;                      /* current program counter */
                                        /* HALT (0) is at address 0 */

/*
 *      generate a single instruction
 */
```

```
int gen(op, mod, val, comment)
        int op;                     /* operation code */
        int mod;                    /* modifier */
        int val;                    /* offset field */
        char * comment;             /* instruction comment */
{
        if (pc >= DIM(prog))
                fatal("Not enough program memory.");
        prog[pc].p_op = op;
        prog[pc].p_mod = mod;
        prog[pc].p_val = val;
        printf("%d:\t%d\t%d,%d\t; %s\n",
                pc, op, mod, val, comment);
        return pc ++;
}
```

The program counter is initialized to one. Location zero in program memory contains zero. As discussed in section 8.1, undefined functions and a return from main() will transfer to address zero and thus halt the simulator.

gen() is the only function which deposits new instructions in program memory. This function is a good place to trace code generation for the simulator. gen() returns the value of the program counter at which the instruction was generated. As we shall see, this is required by some of the other code generation functions; it has no bearing on the calls to gen() made by actions in the parser.

Region modifiers are computed just as before, except that gen_mod() will now deliver the representation as an integer value:

```
int gen_mod(symbol)
        struct symtab * symbol;
{
        switch (symbol->s_blknum) {
        case 1:
                return MOD_GLOBAL;
        case 2:
                return MOD_PARAM;
        }
        return MOD_LOCAL;
}
```

Once we can write program memory with gen(), a number of code generation routines are straightforward to construct, since they are merely calls to gen() with varying calling sequences. These routines could even be defined as macros.

```
gen_alu(mod, comment)
        int mod;                    /* modifier */
        char * comment;             /* instruction comment */
{
        gen(OP_ALU, mod, 0, comment);
}

gen_li(const)
        char * const;               /* Constant value */
{
        gen(OP_LOAD, MOD_IMMED, atoi(const), const);
```

```
        }

gen_pr(op, comment)
        int op;                         /* operation code */
        char * comment;                 /* instruction comment */
{
        gen(op, 0, 0, comment);
}
```

A `Constant` must now be converted into a numerical value to be stored in memory. We use the library function `atoi()` for the conversion; constants must therefore (at least) conform to the syntax expected by this function. Our lexical analyzer pattern for constants actually is more restrictive.

Dealing with forward references poses the only serious problem for in-core code generation. Consider the typical situation:

```
if_prefix
        : IF '(' expression rp
                { $$ = gen_jump(OP_JUMPZ, new_label(), "IF"); }

statement
        : if_prefix statement
                { gen_label($1); }
```

`new_label()` marks the target of the required forward jump; the result is passed to `gen_jump()`. Whatever `gen_jump()` returns is passed over the *yacc* stack to `gen_label()`, which is expected to perform the necessary cleanup, i.e., to resolve the forward branch to reach the present value of pc.

When `gen_jump()` is supposed to create a forward branch, it can generate a branch to a more or less undefined location. The program memory position of this forward branch is returned by `gen_jump()` and handed to `gen_label()`. `gen_label()` simply inserts the current value of the code generation program counter, pc, i.e., the address of the next instruction to be generated, into the offset field of the forward branch, thus resolving it.

The technique works fine for forward labels which are referenced just once, as is the case for control structures. `break` statements, however, and `continue` statements for certain kinds of loops, may cause a forward label to be referenced several times.

Obviously, in general all references to the same undefined label should be chained together, so that `gen_label()` may resolve them all. Since the offset field of a forward branch instruction is unused until `gen_label()` fixes it, it is the convenient place through which to run the chain. The chain can never involve location zero, which means that it can be terminated with a zero value.

In the context of `break` and `continue` we do not know from context whether we deal with forward branches, which must be chained, or with backward branches, which can be resolved immediately. To distinguish both, we will mark unresolved forward branches by chaining them with *negative* indices through program memory.

`gen_jump()` must chain a forward branch, i.e., it must return its memory position as a negative value, and it is convenient for it to return the target of a backward branch:

```
        int gen_jump(op, label, comment)
                int op;                         /* operation code */
                int label;                      /* target of jump */
                char * comment;                 /* instruction comment */
        {       int pc = gen(op, 0, label, comment);

                if (label <= 0)
                        return -pc;     /* new head of chain */
                else
                        return label;   /* already defined */
        }
```

new_label() always marks the end of a chain of forward branches, i.e., it must return zero:

```
        int new_label()
        {
                return 0;               /* end of chain */
        }
```

gen_label() at this point should only be faced with a chain to be resolved. We shall see later that when gen_label() is called in the context of continue, it *might* have nothing to do. Therefore, the argument is inspected; if it is not negative, no chain needs to be fixed:

```
        int gen_label(chain)
                int chain;
        {       int next;

                while (chain < 0)
                {       chain = - chain;
                        next = prog[chain].p_val;
                        if (next > 0)
                                break;  /* already ok */
                        prog[chain].p_val = pc;
                        printf("%d:\t(fixup)\t%d\n", chain, pc);
                        chain = next;
                }
                return pc;
        }
```

gen_label() must return the generated label, i.e., pc, for the implementation of the while statement to be correct:

```
        loop_prefix
                : WHILE '('
                        { $$ = gen_label(new_label());
                          push_continue($$);
                        }
                    expression rp
                        { $$ = $3; }

        statement
                : loop_prefix
                        { $$ = gen_jump(OP_JUMPZ, new_label(), "WHILE");
                          push_break($$);
```

```
                    }
              statement
                    { gen_jump(OP_JUMP, $1, "repeat WHILE");
                      gen_label($2);
                      pop_break();
                      pop_continue();
                    }
```

Let us run through the implementation of while to understand the management of break and continue. At WHILE the continuation point is defined as a new label: new_label() marks it, gen_label() resolves it — there is nothing to be done — and returns the defining address, which is pushed onto the continue stack:

```
        push_continue(label)
                int label;
        {
                c_top = push(c_top, label);
        }
```

Subsequent references to the stack top by continue statements will find a defined label, and thus will result in backward, resolved branches.

Following the loop_prefix in statement, a forward branch to the termination point of the loop is generated: new_label() marks the end of its chain, gen_jump() chains it and returns (negative) its position in memory. The result is placed on the *yacc* stack to be resolved later, and on the break stack for break statements:

```
        push_break(label)
                int label;
        {
                b_top = push(b_top, label);
        }
```

break statements will reference the top of the break stack, find an undefined label, and thus will have to be chained.

Following the entire while statement, a jump is generated to the (defined) continuation point $1. Next, the termination point $2 is defined through a call to gen_label(): since a forward jumpz to this point was coded earlier, it will now be resolved.

We are ready to pop the break stack. Jumps generated by break statements can only be resolved if they have been chained to the stack by gen_break():

```
        gen_break()
        {
                *top(&b_top) = gen_jump(OP_JUMP, *top(&b_top), "BREAK");
        }
```

The chain starts on top of the stack and extends through the forward branches. Another forward branch must be linked into the chain: its position would be returned by gen_jump() and it must replace the element on top of the stack. Since gen_jump() returns the target of a backward (defined) branch, the element on top of the stack would not be changed if it referred to an existing label. Therefore, gen_continue() can be handled identically; both statements are then implemented correctly, regardless of whether the branches are backward or forward:

```
gen_continue()
{
        *top(&c_top) = gen_jump(OP_JUMP, *top(&c_top), "CONTINUE");
}
```

There is one problem, however: we cannot assign to the top element of a stack if the stack is empty. While the other stack management routines are retained from the symbolic code generator, top() is given access to the stack header, so that it may push a dummy element onto an empty stack:

```
static int * top(stack)
        struct bc_stack ** stack;
{
        if (! *stack)
        {       error("no loop open");
                *stack = push(*stack, 0);
        }
        return & (*stack) -> bc_label;
}
```

top() returns a *pointer* to the label entry on top of the stack, so that the entry can be written without knowledge of the stack representation.

Back to popping the break stack: we must resolve undefined branches to the termination point of the loop, i.e., pop_break() must now call gen_label():

```
pop_break()
{
        gen_label(*top(&b_top));
        b_top = pop(b_top);
}
```

gen_label() here serves to resolve forward branches. pop_break() can only be called at the termination point if there are forward references to be resolved.

The chain of branches to the termination point, however, leads to the one jumpz, which was generated following the loop_prefix, and which has already been resolved. This explains why we need to abort the resolving loop in gen_label() at

```
if (next > 0)
```

if we reach a branch on the chain which has already been fixed up.

continue functions in a similar manner to break. The continue stack is therefore popped in an identical fashion, although in this special case no branch needs to be resolved:

```
pop_continue()
{
        gen_label(*top(&c_top));
        c_top = pop(c_top);
}
```

Function calls pose a similar forward reference problem: in C, functions may be used before they are defined. The call instruction is a forward reference in this case. Once the function has been defined, we need to know the location of its entry instruction; subsequent calls to this function can then be resolved immediately.

One popular technique to solve this problem is a *transfer vector*: All calls to functions proceed indirectly through a vector of function addresses, which would be placed in a globally known position, and which would be filled as the entry points become known.

Our technique is more efficient: we chain all forward calls and use gen_label() to resolve them once the entry instruction is generated. The head of the chain, as well as the location of the entry instruction once it is known, can be kept in the s_offset part of the symbol table entry for the function. This component is initialized to be zero, and is thus a suitable end of the chain.

```
gen_call(symbol, count)
        struct symtab * symbol; /* function */
        int     count;          /* # of arguments */
{       int pc;

        chk_parm(symbol, count);
        pc = gen(OP_CALL, count, symbol->s_offset, symbol->s_name);
        if (symbol->s_offset <= 0)
                symbol->s_offset = -pc; /* head of chain */
        while (count-- > 0)
                gen_pr(OP_POP, "pop argument");
        gen(OP_LOAD, MOD_GLOBAL, 0, "push result");
}
```

gen_entry() must resolve any forward references using gen_label() and then define the actual starting address of the function in s_offset. The entry instruction poses a new forward reference problem: it needs to know the size of the local segment, which is not known at the beginning of the function where entry is generated. Once again, we return the address of the incomplete instruction, place it onto the *yacc* value stack, and finally correct things in the fix_entry() function defined below.

```
int gen_entry(symbol)
        struct symtab * symbol; /* function */
{

        symbol->s_offset = gen_label(symbol->s_offset);
        gen(OP_ENTRY, 0, 0, symbol->s_name);
        return symbol->s_offset;
}

fix_entry(symbol, label)
        struct symtab * symbol; /* function */
        int label;
{       extern int l_max;       /* size of local region */

        prog[label].p_val = l_max;
        printf("%d:\tentry\t%d\t; %s\n",
                label, l_max, symbol->s_name);
}
```

Code generation is complete. Once we reach end_program(), we know the size of the generated program segment and the size of the necessary global region, and we can search for the starting address in the symbol table. With this information we can call the simulator:

```
end_program()
{       extern int g_offset;      /* size of global region */
        extern struct symtab * s_find();
        int main = s_find("main") -> s_offset;

        all_program();               /* allocate global variables */
        printf("%d:\tend\t%d,%d\n", pc, g_offset, main);
        simulate(pc, g_offset, main);
}
```

s_find() will always find a symbol table entry for main(); however, if the function has not been defined, s_offset will contain zero. Simulation is then started at address zero, i.e., the simulator is halted immediately.

Whether or not we start the simulator if there were compilation errors can still be decided: the number of errors during compilation, including errors reported with our own error() function, is available in the variable yynerrs. We prefer to start the simulator in any case — we tried to construct it robust enough to at least abort in the presence of run time problems.

8.3 Example

Consider this recursive specification of Euclid's algorithm:

```
/*
 *      Euclid's algorithm (recursively)
 */

main()
{
        gcd(36,54);
}

gcd(a,b)
{
        if (a == b)
                return a;
        else if (a > b)
                return gcd(a-b, b);
        else
                return gcd(a, b-a);
}
```

Execution of the program yields the following result:

```
1:      10      0,0     ; main
2:      4       4,36    ; 36
3:      4       4,54    ; 54
4:      9       2,0     ; gcd
5:      6       0,0     ; pop argument
6:      6       0,0     ; pop argument
7:      4       1,0     ; push result
8:      6       0,0     ; clear stack
9:      11      0,0     ; end of function
1:      entry   0       ; main
4:      (fixup) 10
```

```
10:        10       0,0      ; gcd
11:         4       2,0      ; a
12:         4       2,1      ; b
13:         1      10,0      ; ==
14:         7       0,0      ; IF
15:         4       2,0      ; a
16:         5       1,0      ; save result
17:        11       0,0      ; RETURN
18:         8       0,0      ; past ELSE
14:       (fixup)  19
19:         4       2,0      ; a
20:         4       2,1      ; b
21:         1       7,0      ; >
22:         7       0,0      ; IF
23:         4       2,0      ; a
24:         4       2,1      ; b
25:         1       2,0      ; -
26:         4       2,1      ; b
27:         9       2,10     ; gcd
28:         6       0,0      ; pop argument
29:         6       0,0      ; pop argument
30:         4       1,0      ; push result
31:         5       1,0      ; save result
32:        11       0,0      ; RETURN
33:         8       0,0      ; past ELSE
22:       (fixup)  34
34:         4       2,0      ; a
35:         4       2,1      ; b
36:         4       2,0      ; a
37:         1       2,0      ; -
38:         9       2,10     ; gcd
39:         6       0,0      ; pop argument
40:         6       0,0      ; pop argument
41:         4       1,0      ; push result
42:         5       1,0      ; save result
43:        11       0,0      ; RETURN
33:       (fixup)  44
18:       (fixup)  44
44:        11       0,0      ; end of function
10:       entry     0        ; gcd
45:       end       1,1
```

Execution begins...

```
4:        call    10
14:       jumpz   19
22:       jumpz   34
38:       call    10
14:       jumpz   19
27:       call    10
16:       store    1,0      to 18
17:       return  18 to 28
31:       store    1,0      to 18
32:       return  18 to 39
42:       store    1,0      to 18
43:       return  18 to 5
```

```
9:        return  18 to 0
0:        halt
```

The example shows nicely that the code could be shortened by postprocessing, since, e.g., of a series of return instructions only the first can actually be reached.

8.4 Problems

1. Improve the simulator by having return pass result values on the stack, and by eliminating from gen_call() the pop and load instructions following call. (See section 8.1.)

2. As was mentioned, the call, return, and entry instructions for our fictitious machine are not very realistic. On real machines, these instructions tend to be much simpler. Design more "realistic" instructions, and change the code generator and the simulator to use them. Hint: you will probably need some register manipulation instructions.

3. Add run-time options to the simulator, either through compiler options or by special comments which generate appropriate pseudo-instructions. Possible options include: printing or suppressing a listing of the compiled code before execution begins; an option of whether to execute the program, based on the presence or absence of compilation errors, or on the number or type of errors (ordinary errors, or warnings); a limit on the number of instructions to be simulated; a more extensive trace option, perhaps with a limit to the number or type of instructions to be traced.

4. Modify the simulator to handle arithmetic exceptions, such as division by zero.

5. Modify the simulator to use dynamically managed memory, rather than the fixed-size arrays of "tunable size" defined near the beginning of this chapter.

6. The program segment structure, defined near the beginning of this chapter to simplify decoding, is neither realistic of ordinary machine architecture, nor particularly compact. Modify this feature of the simulator to make it more efficient and more realistic.

8.5 Projects

1. Reorganize the compiler so that it consists of several separate programs: (1) the compiler of chapter 7, which generates assembler code; (2) a simple assembler (the assembler can, of course, be written using *yacc* and *lex*!); and (3) the simulator.

2. Using the three programs of the previous project, rearrange the compiler so that functions can be compiled separately, and the results combined either by the assembler or by a separate linking loader. Note that global variables might be included in any function compilation, and all must appear in the final executed program.

3. A large number of language extensions is conceivable: char or other integer-type variables, floating point variables, vectors with or without pointers, structures; other control features, such as switch, for, do while.

4. More interesting language extensions result from introducing parallelism, e.g., by introducing standard procedures (i.e., simulator instructions) for coroutine jumps in the style of Modula-2, or by adding a parallel control structure. Vectors should be added also, to make this project more realistic.

The individual chapters document mostly changes to the compiler. This appendix contains a complete listing to permit a review of the final system in context.

A.1 Syntax analysis

samplec.y is the file from which *yacc* produces the recognizer. As the compiler is developed through recognition, error recovery, semantic analysis, and synthesis, this file has to be extended. The listing shows the final version for code generation. This is also the final version for simulation, as long as the C preprocessor statement

```
#include "gen.h"
```

is replaced by

```
#include "sim.h"
```

The two header files provide identical names, but with quite different definitions.

samplec.y

```
/*
 *       sample c
 *       syntax analysis with error recovery
 *       symbol table
 *       memory allocation
 *       code generation
 *       (s/r conflicts: one on ELSE, one on error)
 */

%{
#include "symtab.h"        /* symbol table mnemonics */
#include "gen.h"           /* code generation mnemonics */

#define OFFSET(x)          ( ((struct symtab *) x) -> s_offset )
#define NAME(x)            ( ((struct symtab *) x) -> s_name )

extern int l_offset, l_max;
%}

%union  {
        struct symtab * y_sym;  /* Identifier */
        char * y_str;           /* Constant */
        int y_num;              /* count */
        int y_lab;              /* label */
        }

/*
 *       terminal symbols
 */

%token  <y_sym> Identifier
%token  <y_str> Constant
```

```
        %token   INT
        %token   IF
        %token   ELSE
        %token   WHILE
        %token   BREAK
        %token   CONTINUE
        %token   RETURN
        %token   ';'
        %token   '('
        %token   ')'
        %token   '{'
        %token   '}'
        %token   '+'
        %token   '-'
        %token   '*'
        %token   '/'
        %token   '%'
        %token   '>'
        %token   '<'
        %token   GE        /* >= */
        %token   LE        /* <= */
        %token   EQ        /* == */
        %token   NE        /* != */
        %token   '&'
        %token   '^'
        %token   '|'
        %token   '='
        %token   PE        /* += */
        %token   ME        /* -= */
        %token   TE        /* *= */
        %token   DE        /* /= */
        %token   RE        /* %= */
        %token   PP        /* ++ */
        %token   MM        /* -- */
        %token   ','

    /*
     *      typed non-terminal symbols
     */

    %type    <y_sym> optional_parameter_list, parameter_list
    %type    <y_num> optional_argument_list, argument_list
    %type    <y_lab> if_prefix, loop_prefix

    /*
     *      precedence table
     */

    %right   '=' PE ME TE DE RE
    %left    '|'
    %left    '^'
    %left    '&'
    %left    EQ NE
    %left    '<' '>' GE LE
    %left    '+' '-'
    %left    '*' '/' '%'
```

```
        %right  PP MM

        %%

        program
                :           { init(); }
                  definitions
                          { end_program(); }

        definitions
                : definition
                | definitions definition
                        { yyerrok; }
                | error
                | definitions error

        definition
                : function_definition
                | INT function_definition
                | declaration

        function_definition
                : Identifier '('
                        { make_func($1);
                          blk_push();
                        }
                  optional_parameter_list rp
                  parameter_declarations
                        { chk_parm($1, parm_default($4));
                          all_parm($4);
                          l_max = 0;
                          $<y_lab>$ = gen_entry($1);
                        }
                  compound_statement
                        { all_func($1);
                          gen_pr(OP_RETURN, "end of function");
                          fix_entry($1, $<y_lab>7);
                        }

        optional_parameter_list
                : /* no formal parameters */
                        { $$ = (struct symtab *) 0; }
                | parameter_list
                        /* $$ = $1 = chain of formal parameters */

        parameter_list
                : Identifier
                        { $$ = link_parm($1, (struct symtab *) 0); }
                | Identifier ',' parameter_list
                        { $$ = link_parm($1, $3);
                          yyerrok;
                        }
                | error
                        { $$ = 0; }
                | error parameter_list
                        { $$ = $2; }
```

```
        | Identifier error parameter_list
              { $$ = link_parm($1, $3); }
        | error ',' parameter_list
              { $$ = $3;
                yyerrok;
              }

parameter_declarations
        : /* null */
        | parameter_declarations parameter_declaration
              { yyerrok; }
        | parameter_declarations error

parameter_declaration
        : INT parameter_declarator_list sc

parameter_declarator_list
        : Identifier
              { make_parm($1); }
        | parameter_declarator_list ',' Identifier
              { make_parm($3);
                yyerrok;
              }
        | error
        | parameter_declarator_list error
        | parameter_declarator_list error Identifier
              { make_parm($3);
                yyerrok;
              }
        | parameter_declarator_list ',' error

compound_statement
        : '{'
              { $<y_lab>$ = l_offset;
                blk_push();
              }
          declarations statements rr
              { if (l_offset > l_max)
                      l_max = l_offset;
                l_offset = $<y_lab>2;
                blk_pop();
              }

declarations
        : /* null */
        | declarations declaration
              { yyerrok; }
        | declarations error

declaration
        : INT declarator_list sc

declarator_list
        : Identifier
              { all_var($1); }
        | declarator_list ',' Identifier
```

```
                        { all_var($3);
                          yyerrok;
                        }
              | error
              | declarator_list error
              | declarator_list error Identifier
                        { all_var($3);
                          yyerrok;
                        }
              | declarator_list ',' error

statements
              : /* null */
              | statements statement
                        { yyerrok; }
              | statements error

statement
              : expression sc
                        { gen_pr(OP_POP, "clear stack"); }
              | sc
              | BREAK sc
                        { gen_break(); }
              | CONTINUE sc
                        { gen_continue(); }
              | RETURN sc
                        { gen_pr(OP_RETURN, "RETURN"); }
              | RETURN expression sc
                        { gen(OP_STORE, MOD_GLOBAL, 0, "save result");
                          gen_pr(OP_RETURN, "RETURN");
                        }
              | compound_statement
              | if_prefix statement
                        { gen_label($1); }
              | if_prefix statement ELSE
                        { $<y_lab>$ = gen_jump(OP_JUMP, new_label(),
                                "past ELSE");
                          gen_label($1);
                        }
                statement
                        { gen_label($<y_lab>4); }
              | loop_prefix
                        { $<y_lab>$ = gen_jump(OP_JUMPZ, new_label(),
                                "WHILE");
                          push_break($<y_lab>$);
                        }
                statement
                        { gen_jump(OP_JUMP, $1, "repeat WHILE");
                          gen_label($<y_lab>2);
                          pop_break();
                          pop_continue();
                        }

if_prefix
              : IF '(' expression rp
                        { $$ = gen_jump(OP_JUMPZ, new_label(), "IF"); }
```

```
                    | IF error
                            { $$ = gen_jump(OP_JUMPZ, new_label(), "IF"); }

        loop_prefix
                : WHILE '('
                            { $<y_lab>$ = gen_label(new_label());
                              push_continue($<y_lab>$);
                            }
                  expression rp
                            { $$ = $<y_lab>3; }
                | WHILE error
                            { $$ = gen_label(new_label());
                              push_continue($$);
                            }

        expression
                : binary
                | expression ','
                            { gen_pr(OP_POP, "discard"); }
                  binary
                            { yyerrok; }
                | error ',' binary
                            { yyerrok; }
                | expression error
                | expression ',' error

        binary
                : Identifier
                            { chk_var($1);
                              gen(OP_LOAD, gen_mod($1), OFFSET($1), NAME($1));
                            }
                | Constant
                            { gen_li($1); }
                | '(' expression rp
                | '(' error rp
                | Identifier '('
                            { chk_func($1); }
                  optional_argument_list rp
                            { gen_call($1,$4); }
                | PP Identifier
                            { chk_var($2);
                              gen(OP_INC, gen_mod($2), OFFSET($2), NAME($2));
                            }
                | MM Identifier
                            { chk_var($2);
                              gen(OP_DEC, gen_mod($2), OFFSET($2), NAME($2));
                            }
                | binary '+' binary
                            { gen_alu(ALU_ADD, "+"); }
                | binary '-' binary
                            { gen_alu(ALU_SUB, "-"); }
                | binary '*' binary
                            { gen_alu(ALU_MUL, "*"); }
                | binary '/' binary
                            { gen_alu(ALU_DIV, "/"); }
                | binary '%' binary
```

```
                  { gen_alu(ALU_MOD, "%"); }
        | binary '>' binary
                  { gen_alu(ALU_GT, ">"); }
        | binary '<' binary
                  { gen_alu(ALU_LT, "<"); }
        | binary GE binary
                  { gen_alu(ALU_GE, ">="); }
        | binary LE binary
                  { gen_alu(ALU_LE, "<="); }
        | binary EQ binary
                  { gen_alu(ALU_EQ, "=="); }
        | binary NE binary
                  { gen_alu(ALU_NE, "!="); }
        | binary '&' binary
                  { gen_alu(ALU_AND, "&"); }
        | binary '^' binary
                  { gen_alu(ALU_XOR, "^"); }
        | binary '|' binary
                  { gen_alu(ALU_OR, "|"); }
        | Identifier '=' binary
                  { chk_var($1);
                    gen(OP_STORE, gen_mod($1), OFFSET($1), NAME($1));
                  }
        | Identifier PE
                  { chk_var($1);
                    gen(OP_LOAD, gen_mod($1), OFFSET($1), NAME($1));
                  }
          binary
                  { gen_alu(ALU_ADD, "+");
                    gen(OP_STORE, gen_mod($1), OFFSET($1), NAME($1));
                  }
        | Identifier ME
                  { chk_var($1);
                    gen(OP_LOAD, gen_mod($1), OFFSET($1), NAME($1));
                  }
          binary
                  { gen_alu(ALU_SUB, "-");
                    gen(OP_STORE, gen_mod($1), OFFSET($1), NAME($1));
                  }
        | Identifier TE
                  { chk_var($1);
                    gen(OP_LOAD, gen_mod($1), OFFSET($1), NAME($1));
                  }
          binary
                  { gen_alu(ALU_MUL, "*");
                    gen(OP_STORE, gen_mod($1), OFFSET($1), NAME($1));
                  }
        | Identifier DE
                  { chk_var($1);
                    gen(OP_LOAD, gen_mod($1), OFFSET($1), NAME($1));
                  }
          binary
                  { gen_alu(ALU_DIV, "/");
                    gen(OP_STORE, gen_mod($1), OFFSET($1), NAME($1));
                  }
        | Identifier RE
```

```
                        { chk_var($1);
                          gen(OP_LOAD, gen_mod($1), OFFSET($1), NAME($1));
                        }
                binary
                        { gen_alu(ALU_MOD, "%");
                          gen(OP_STORE, gen_mod($1), OFFSET($1), NAME($1));
                        }

        optional_argument_list
                : /* no actual arguments */
                        { $$ = 0; }
                | argument_list
                        /* $$ = $1 = # of actual arguments */

        argument_list
                : binary
                        { $$ = 1; }
                | argument_list ',' binary
                        { ++ $$;
                          yyerrok;
                        }
                | error
                        { $$ = 0; }
                | argument_list error
                | argument_list ',' error

        /*
         *      make certain terminal symbols very important
         */

        rp      : ')'    { yyerrok; }
        sc      : ';'    { yyerrok; }
        rr      : '}'    { yyerrok; }
```

A parser is then prepared with the following command:

```
yacc -d samplec.y
```

The $-d$ option instructs *yacc* to produce both the parser *y.tab.c* and the token definition file *y.tab.h*.

A.2 Lexical analysis

The lexical analyzer function in file *samplec.l* was shown in section 2.7. From this file, the lexical analyzer is prepared with the following command:

```
lex samplec.l
```

A.3 Messages

File *message.c* contains the C functions introduced in chapter 5 to issue error messages. (The comments /*VARARGS1*/ prevent *lint* from complaining about the varying number of arguments with which these functions are called.)

message.c

```
/*
 *       message routines
 */

#include <stdio.h>

#define VARARG   fmt, v1, v2, v3, v4, v5
#define VARPARM  (VARARG) char * fmt;

extern FILE * yyerfp;

                                /*VARARGS1*/
message VARPARM
{
        yywhere();
        fprintf(yyerfp, VARARG);
        putc('\n', yyerfp);
}

                                /*VARARGS1*/
error VARPARM
{       extern int yynerrs;

        fprintf(yyerfp, "[error %d] ", ++ yynerrs);
        message(VARARG);
}

                                /*VARARGS1*/
warning VARPARM
{
        fputs("[warning] ", yyerfp);
        message(VARARG);
}

                                /*VARARGS1*/
fatal VARPARM
{
        fputs("[fatal error] ", yyerfp);
        message(VARARG);
        exit(1);
}

                                /*VARARGS1*/
bug VARPARM
{
        fputs("BUG: ", yyerfp);
        message(VARARG);
        exit(1);
}
```

message.c is a good place for the strsave() function, if it is not already available in the local library. Another suitable place for it is the library described in section A.8. Here is a definition for strsave():

```
char * strsave(s)
        register char * s;
{       register char * cp = calloc(strlen(s)+1, 1);

        if (cp)
        {       strcpy(cp, s);
                return cp;
        }
        fatal("No more room to save strings.");
}
```

A.4 Symbol table routines

File *symtab.h* contains the symbol table mnemonics required to compile *samplec.y*.

symtab.h

```
/*
 *      sample c -- header file for symbol table
 */

struct symtab {
        char *  s_name;         /* name pointer */
        int     s_type;         /* symbol type */
        int     s_blknum;       /* static block depth */
        union {                 /* multi-purpose */
                int s__num;
                struct symtab * s__link;
                } s__;
        int     s_offset;       /* symbol definition */
        struct symtab * s_next; /* next entry */
        };

#define s_pnum  s__.s__num      /* count of parameters */
#define NOT_SET (-1)            /* no count yet set */
#define s_plist s__.s__link     /* chain of parameters */

/*
 *      s_type values
 */

#define UDEC    0       /* not declared */
#define FUNC    1       /* function */
#define UFUNC   2       /* undefined function */
#define VAR     3       /* declared variable */
#define PARM    4       /* undeclared parameter */

/*
 *      s_type values for S_TRACE
 */

#define SYMmap  "undeclared", "function", "undefined function", \
                "variable", "parameter"

/*
 *      typed functions, symbol table module
```

```
        */

        struct symtab * link_parm();     /* chain parameters */
        struct symtab * s_find();        /* locate symbol by name */
        struct symtab * make_parm();     /* declare parameter */
        struct symtab * make_var();      /* define variable */
        struct symtab * make_func();     /* define function */


        /*
         *      typed library functions
         */

        char * strsave();                /* dynamically save a string */
        char * calloc();                 /* dynamically obtain memory */
```

File *symtab.c* contains the C functions for manipulation of the symbol table, as introduced in chapter 5.

symtab.c

```
        /*
         *      sample c -- symbol table definition and manipulation
         */

        #include "symtab.h"
        #include "y.tab.h"


        /*
         *      symbol table
         */

        static   struct   symtab
                symtab,                  /* blind element */
                * s_gbl;                 /* global end of chain */
        #define s_lcl    (& symtab)      /* local end of chain */


        /*
         *      block table
         */

        static int blknum = 0;           /* current static block depth */


        /*
         *      add a new name to local region
         */

        static struct symtab * s_create(name)
                register char * name;
        {       register struct symtab * new_entry = (struct symtab *)
                                calloc(1, sizeof(struct symtab));

                if (new_entry)
                {       new_entry->s_next = s_lcl->s_next;
                        s_lcl->s_next = new_entry;
                        new_entry->s_name = strsave(name);
                        new_entry->s_type = UDEC;
                        new_entry->s_blknum = 0;
```

```
                            new_entry->s_pnum = NOT_SET;
                            return new_entry;
                    }
                fatal("No more room for symbols.");
                /*NOTREACHED*/
        }


        /*
         *      move an entry from local to global region
         */

        static s_move(symbol)
                register struct symtab * symbol;
        {       register struct symtab * ptr;

                /* find desired entry in symtab chain (bug if missing) */
                for (ptr = s_lcl; ptr->s_next != symbol; ptr = ptr->s_next)
                        if (! ptr->s_next)
                                bug("s_move");

                /* unlink it from its present position */
                ptr->s_next = symbol->s_next;

                /* relink at global end of symtab */
                s_gbl->s_next = symbol;
                s_gbl = symbol;
                s_gbl->s_next = (struct symtab *) 0;
        }

        /*
         *      initialize symbol and block table
         */

        init()
        {
                blk_push();
                s_gbl = s_create("main");
                s_gbl->s_type = UFUNC;
        }

        /*
         *      push block table
         */

        blk_push()
        {
                ++ blknum;
        }

        /*
         *      locate entry by name
         */

        struct symtab * s_find(name)
                char * name;
        {       register struct symtab * ptr;
```

```
                /* search symtab until match or end of symtab chain */
                for (ptr = s_lcl->s_next; ptr; ptr = ptr->s_next)
                        if (! ptr->s_name)
                                bug("s_find");
                        else
                                /* return ptr if names match */
                                if (strcmp(ptr->s_name, name) == 0)
                                        return ptr;
                /* search fails, return NULL */
                return (struct symtab *) 0;
}


/*
 *      interface for lexical analyzer:
 *      locate or enter Identifier, save text of Constant
 */


s_lookup(yylex)
        int yylex;                      /* Constant or Identifier */
{       extern char yytext[];   /* text of symbol */

        switch (yylex) {
        case Constant:
                yylval.y_str = strsave(yytext);
                break;
        case Identifier:
                if (yylval.y_sym = s_find(yytext))
                        break;
                yylval.y_sym = s_create(yytext);
                break;
        default:
                bug("s_lookup");
        }
}


/*
 *      mark entry as part of parameter_list
 */


struct symtab * link_parm(symbol, next)
        register struct symtab * symbol, * next;
{
        switch (symbol->s_type) {
        case PARM:
                error("duplicate parameter %s", symbol->s_name);
                return next;
        case FUNC:
        case UFUNC:
        case VAR:
                symbol = s_create(symbol->s_name);
        case UDEC:
                break;
        default:
                bug("link_parm");
        }
        symbol->s_type = PARM;
```

```
                        symbol->s_blknum = blknum;
                        symbol->s_plist = next;
                        return symbol;
        }


        /*
         *      declare a parameter
         */

        struct symtab * make_parm(symbol)
                register struct symtab * symbol;
        {
                switch (symbol->s_type) {
                case VAR:
                        if (symbol->s_blknum == 2)
                        {       error("parameter %s declared twice",
                                        symbol->s_name);
                                return symbol;
                        }
                case UDEC:
                case FUNC:
                case UFUNC:
                        error("%s is not a parameter", symbol->s_name);
                        symbol = s_create(symbol->s_name);
                case PARM:
                        break;
                default:
                        bug("make_parm");
                }
                symbol->s_type = VAR;
                symbol->s_blknum = blknum;
                return symbol;
        }


        /*
         *      define a variable
         */

        struct symtab * make_var(symbol)
                register struct symtab * symbol;
        {
                switch (symbol->s_type) {
                case VAR:
                case FUNC:
                case UFUNC:
                        if (symbol->s_blknum == blknum
                            || symbol->s_blknum == 2 && blknum == 3)
                                error("duplicate name %s", symbol->s_name);
                        symbol = s_create(symbol->s_name);
                case UDEC:
                        break;
                case PARM:
                        error("unexpected parameter %s", symbol->s_name);
                        break;
                default:
                        bug("make_var");
```

```
                }
                symbol->s_type = VAR;
                symbol->s_blknum = blknum;
                return symbol;
        }


        /*
         *      define a function
         */

        struct symtab * make_func(symbol)
                register struct symtab * symbol;
        {
                switch (symbol->s_type) {
                case UFUNC:
                case UDEC:
                        break;
                case VAR:
                        error("function name %s same as global variable",
                                symbol->s_name);
                        return symbol;
                case FUNC:
                        error("duplicate function definition %s",
                                symbol->s_name);
                        return symbol;
                default:
                        bug("make_func");
                }
                symbol->s_type = FUNC;
                symbol->s_blknum = 1;
                return symbol;
        }


        /*
         *      set or verify number of parameters
         */

        chk_parm(symbol, count)
                register struct symtab * symbol;
                register int count;
        {
                if (symbol->s_pnum == NOT_SET)
                        symbol->s_pnum = count;
                else if ((int) symbol->s_pnum != count)
                        warning("function %s should have %d argument(s)",
                                symbol->s_name, symbol->s_pnum);
        }


        /*
         *      default undeclared parameters, count
         */

        int parm_default(symbol)
                register struct symtab * symbol;
        {       register int count = 0;
```

```
            while (symbol)
            {       ++ count;
                    if (symbol->s_type == PARM)
                            symbol->s_type = VAR;
                    symbol = symbol->s_plist;
            }
            return count;
    }


    /*
     *      pop block table
     */

    blk_pop()
    {       register struct symtab * ptr;

            for (ptr = s_lcl->s_next;
                 ptr &&
                 (ptr->s_blknum >= blknum || ptr->s_blknum == 0);
                 ptr = s_lcl->s_next)
            {
                    if (! ptr->s_name)
                            bug("blk_pop null name");
    #ifdef TRACE
                    {       static char * type[] = { SYMmap };

                            message("Popping %s: %s, depth %d, offset %d",
                                    ptr->s_name, type[ptr->s_type],
                                    ptr->s_blknum, ptr->s_offset);
                    }
    #endif TRACE
                    if (ptr->s_type == UFUNC)
                            error("undefined function %s",
                                    ptr->s_name);
                    cfree(ptr->s_name);
                    s_lcl->s_next = ptr->s_next;
                    cfree(ptr);
            }
            -- blknum;
    }


    /*
     *      check reference or assignment to variable
     */

    chk_var(symbol)
            register struct symtab * symbol;
    {
            switch (symbol->s_type) {
            case UDEC:
                    error("undeclared variable %s", symbol->s_name);
                    break;
            case PARM:
                    error("unexpected parameter %s", symbol->s_name);
                    break;
            case FUNC:
```

```
                case UFUNC:
                        error("function %s used as variable",
                                symbol->s_name);
                case VAR:
                        return;
                default:
                        bug("check_var");
                }
        symbol->s_type = VAR;
        symbol->s_blknum = blknum;
}


/*
 *      check reference to function, implicitly declare it
 */


chk_func(symbol)
        register struct symtab * symbol;
{
        switch (symbol->s_type) {
        case UDEC:
                break;
        case PARM:
                error("unexpected parameter %s", symbol->s_name);
                symbol->s_pnum = NOT_SET;
                return;
        case VAR:
                error("variable %s used as function",
                        symbol->s_name);
                symbol->s_pnum = NOT_SET;
        case UFUNC:
        case FUNC:
                return;
        default:
                bug("check_func");
        }
        s_move(symbol);
        symbol->s_type = UFUNC;
        symbol->s_blknum = 1;
}
```

A.5 Memory allocation

The C functions for memory allocation, introduced in chapter 6, are contained in file *mem.c*.

mem.c

```
/*
 *      sample c -- memory allocation
 */


#include "symtab.h"

/*
 *      global counters
```

```
        */

int     g_offset = 1,            /* offset in global region */
        l_offset = 0,            /* offset in local region */
        l_max;                   /* size of local region */


/*
 *      allocate a (global or local) variable
 */

all_var(symbol)
        register struct symtab * symbol;
{       extern struct symtab * make_var();

        symbol = make_var(symbol);

        /* if not in parameter region, assign suitable offset */
        switch (symbol->s_blknum) {
        default:                            /* local region */
                symbol->s_offset = l_offset++;
        case 2:                             /* parameter region */
                break;
        case 1:                             /* global region */
                symbol->s_offset = g_offset++;
                break;
        case 0:
                bug("all_var");
        }
}


/*
 *      complete allocation
 */

all_program()
{
        blk_pop();

#ifdef  TRACE
        message("global region has %d word(s)", g_offset);
#endif
}


/*
 *      allocate all parameters
 */

all_parm(symbol)
        register struct symtab * symbol;
{       register int p_offset = 0;

        while (symbol)
        {       symbol->s_offset = p_offset ++;
                symbol = symbol->s_plist;
        }
```

```
        #ifdef   TRACE
                 message("parameter region has %d word(s)", p_offset);
        #endif
        }

        /*
         *       complete allocation of a function
         */

        all_func(symbol)
                 struct symtab * symbol;
        {
                 blk_pop();

        #ifdef   TRACE
                 message("local region has %d word(s)", l_max);
        #endif
        }
```

A.6 Code generation

File *gen.h* includes the mnemonics for symbolic code generation required in the compilation of *samplec.y*.

gen.h

```
        /*
         *       sample c -- header file for code generation
         */

        /*
         *       operation codes for pseudo machine
         */

        #define OP_ALU      "alu"        /* arithmetic-logic-op  */
        #define OP_DEC      "dec"        /* region,offset        */
        #define OP_INC      "inc"        /* region,offset        */
        #define OP_LOAD     "load"       /* region,offset        */
        #define OP_STORE    "store"      /* region,offset        */
        #define OP_POP      "pop"        /*                      */
        #define OP_JUMPZ    "jumpz"      /* label                */
        #define OP_JUMP     "jump"       /* label                */
        #define OP_CALL     "call"       /* parm-count,address   */
        #define OP_ENTRY    "entry"      /* local-frame-size     */
        #define OP_RETURN   "return"     /*                      */

        /*
         *       region modifiers
         */

        #define MOD_GLOBAL  "gbl"        /* global region        */
        #define MOD_PARAM   "par"        /* parameter region     */
        #define MOD_LOCAL   "lcl"        /* local region         */
        #define MOD_IMMED   "con"        /* load only: Constant  */

        /*
```

```
*       OP_ALU modifiers
*/

#define ALU_ADD "+"              /* addition           */
#define ALU_SUB "-"              /* subtraction        */
#define ALU_MUL "*"              /* multiplication     */
#define ALU_DIV "/"              /* division           */
#define ALU_MOD "%"              /* remainder          */
#define ALU_LT  "<"              /* compares as: <     */
#define ALU_GT  ">"              /*              >      */
#define ALU_LE  "<="             /*              <=     */
#define ALU_GE  ">="             /*              >=     */
#define ALU_EQ  "=="             /*              ==     */
#define ALU_NE  "!="             /*              !=     */
#define ALU_AND "&"              /* bit-wise and       */
#define ALU_OR  "|"              /* bit-wise or        */
#define ALU_XOR "^"              /* bit-wise excl. or  */

/*
*       typed functions, code generator
*/

char * gen_mod();               /* region modifier */
```

File *gen.c* includes the C functions which generate assembler code for our fictitious *sampleC* machine. These routines were introduced in chapter 7.

gen.c

```
/*
*       sample c -- code generation
*/

#include "symtab.h"
#include "gen.h"

/*
*       generate various instruction formats
*/

gen_alu(mod, comment)
        char * mod;             /* mnemonic modifier */
        char * comment;         /* instruction comment */
{
        printf("\t%s\t%s\t\t; %s\n", OP_ALU, mod, comment);
}

gen_li(const)
        char * const;           /* Constant value */
{
        printf("\t%s\t%s,%s\n", OP_LOAD, MOD_IMMED, const);
}

char * gen_mod(symbol)
        struct symtab * symbol;
{
        switch (symbol->s_blknum) {
```

```
                case 1:
                        return MOD_GLOBAL;
                case 2:
                        return MOD_PARAM;
                }
                return MOD_LOCAL;
}

gen(op, mod, val, comment)
        char * op;                      /* mnemonic operation code */
        char * mod;                     /* mnemonic modifier */
        int val;                        /* offset field */
        char * comment;                 /* instruction comment */
{
        printf("\t%s\t%s,%d\t\t; %s\n", op, mod, val, comment);
}

gen_pr(op, comment)
        char * op;                      /* mnemonic operation code */
        char * comment;                 /* instruction comment */
{
        printf("\t%s\t\t\t; %s\n", op, comment);
}

/*
 *      generate printable internal label
 */

#define LABEL   "$$%d"

static char * format_label(label)
        int label;
{       static char buffer[sizeof LABEL + 2];

        sprintf(buffer, LABEL, label);
        return buffer;
}

/*
 *      generate jumps, return target
 */

int gen_jump(op, label, comment)
        char * op;                      /* mnemonic operation code */
        int label;                      /* target of jump */
        char * comment;                 /* instruction comment */
{
        printf("\t%s\t%s\t\t; %s\n", op, format_label(label),
                comment);
        return label;
}

/*
 *      generate unique internal label
 */
```

```c
int new_label()
{       static int next_label = 0;

        return ++next_label;
}

/*
 *      define internal label
 */

int gen_label(label)
        int label;
{
        printf("%s\tequ\t*\n", format_label(label));
        return label;
}

/*
 *      label stack manager
 */

static struct bc_stack {
        int bc_label;           /* label from new_label */
        struct bc_stack * bc_next;
        } * b_top,              /* head of break stack */
          * c_top;              /* head of continue stack */

static struct bc_stack * push(stack, label)
        struct bc_stack * stack;
        int label;
{       struct bc_stack * new_entry = (struct bc_stack *)
                calloc(1, sizeof(struct bc_stack));

        if (new_entry)
        {       new_entry->bc_next = stack;
                new_entry->bc_label = label;
                return new_entry;
        }
        fatal("No more room to compile loops.");
        /*NOTREACHED*/
}

static struct bc_stack * pop(stack)
        struct bc_stack * stack;
{       struct bc_stack * old_entry;

        if (stack)
        {       old_entry = stack;
                stack = old_entry->bc_next;
                cfree(old_entry);
                return stack;
        }
        bug("break/continue stack underflow");
        /*NOTREACHED*/
}
```

```
static int top(stack)
        struct bc_stack * stack;
{
        if (! stack)
        {       error("no loop open");
                return 0;
        }
        else
                return stack->bc_label;
}

/*
 *      BREAK and CONTINUE
 */

push_break(label)
        int label;
{
        b_top = push(b_top, label);
}

push_continue(label)
        int label;
{
        c_top = push(c_top, label);
}

pop_break()
{
        b_top = pop(b_top);
}

pop_continue()
{
        c_top = pop(c_top);
}

gen_break()
{
        gen_jump(OP_JUMP, top(b_top), "BREAK");
}

gen_continue()
{
        gen_jump(OP_JUMP, top(c_top), "CONTINUE");
}

/*
 *      function call
 */

gen_call(symbol, count)
        struct symtab * symbol; /* function */
        int count;                      /* # of arguments */
{
        chk_parm(symbol, count);
```

```
          printf("\t%s\t%d,%s\n", OP_CALL, count, symbol->s_name);
          while (count-- > 0)
                  gen_pr(OP_POP, "pop argument");
          gen(OP_LOAD, MOD_GLOBAL, 0, "push result");
}


/*
 *        function prologue
 */

int gen_entry(symbol)
          struct symtab * symbol; /* function */
{         int label = new_label();

          printf("%s\t", symbol->s_name);
          printf("%s\t%s\n", OP_ENTRY, format_label(label));
          return label;
}

fix_entry(symbol, label)
          struct symtab * symbol; /* function */
          int label;
{         extern int l_max;        /* size of local region */

          printf("%s\tequ\t%d\t\t; %s\n", format_label(label),
                  l_max, symbol->s_name);
}

/*
 *        wrap-up
 */

end_program()
{         extern int g_offset;     /* size of global region */

          all_program();           /* allocate global variables */
          printf("\tend\t%d,main\n", g_offset);
}
```

The code generator for our fictitious machine language can be compiled using the following command:

```
cc gen.c mem.c symtab.c message.c y.tab.c lex.yy.c \
        colib -ll -o gen
```

colib contains the *yacc* support functions explained in section A.8.

A.7 A load-and-go system

File *sim.h* replaces *gen.h* in the compilation of *samplec.y* to make the load-and-go version of the *sampleC* compiler. It defines the same mnemonics as *gen.h*, but gives them definitions needed by the simulator.

sim.h

```
/*
 *      sample c -- header file for simulation
 */


/*
 *      operation codes for pseudo machine
 */

#define OP_ALU    1      /* alu   arithmetic-logic-op   */
#define OP_DEC    2      /* dec   region,offset         */
#define OP_INC    3      /* inc   region,offset         */
#define OP_LOAD   4      /* load  region,offset         */
#define OP_STORE  5      /* store region,offset         */
#define OP_POP    6      /* pop                         */
#define OP_JUMPZ  7      /* jumpz label                 */
#define OP_JUMP   8      /* jump  label                 */
#define OP_CALL   9      /* call  routine-address       */
#define OP_ENTRY 10      /* entry local-frame-size      */
#define OP_RETURN 11     /* return                      */


/*
 *      region modifiers
 */

#define MOD_GLOBAL 1      /* global region      */
#define MOD_PARAM  2      /* parameter region   */
#define MOD_LOCAL  3      /* local region       */
#define MOD_IMMED  4      /* load only: Constant */


/*
 *      OP_ALU modifiers
 */

#define ALU_ADD 1         /* addition           */
#define ALU_SUB 2         /* subtraction        */
#define ALU_MUL 3         /* multiplication     */
#define ALU_DIV 4         /* division           */
#define ALU_MOD 5         /* remainder          */
#define ALU_LT  6         /* compares as: <     */
#define ALU_GT  7         /*              >     */
#define ALU_LE  8         /*              <=    */
#define ALU_GE  9         /*              >=    */
#define ALU_EQ  10        /*              ==    */
#define ALU_NE  11        /*              !=    */
#define ALU_AND 12        /* bit-wise and       */
#define ALU_OR  13        /* bit-wise or        */
#define ALU_XOR 14        /* bit-wise excl. or  */


/*
 *      program memory structure
 */

struct prog {
        short p_op;       /* operation code */
```

```
            short p_mod;    /* modifier */
            int p_val;      /* offset or other value */
            };

    /*
     *      tunable limits
     */

    #define L_PROG  200     /* max. program size */
    #define L_DATA  100     /* max. area for stack, etc. */
    #define DIM(x)  (sizeof x / sizeof x[0]) /* extent */
```

File *sim.c* contains the actual simulator for our fictitious machine, as introduced in chapter 8.

sim.c

```
    /*
     *      sample c -- machine simulator
     */

    #include "sim.h"

    /*
     *      data and program memory
     */

    static int data[L_DATA];
    extern struct prog prog[];

    /*
     *      registers
     */

    static struct prog * inst;      /* -> current instruction */
    #define G        0              /* global segment */
    static int P;                   /* current parameter segment */
    static int L;                   /* current local segment */
    static int T;                   /* top of stack */

    /*
     *      shorthand notations
     */

    #define TOP     data[T-1]       /* right operand: top of stack */
    #define NEXT    data[T-2]       /* left operand: below TOP */
    #define PUSH    data[T++]       /* new cell to come onto stack */
    #define POP     -- T            /* -> discarded cell from stack */
    #define MEMORY  data[address()] /* effectively addressed cell */
    #define RESULT  data[G]         /* result value of function */

    /*
     *      address decoder
     */

    static int address()    /* effective current data address */
    {       register int ad;
```

```
                switch (inst->p_mod) {
                case MOD_GLOBAL:
                        ad = G;
                        break;
                case MOD_PARAM:
                        ad = P;
                        break;
                case MOD_LOCAL:
                        ad = L;
                        break;
                default:
                        bug("invalid p_mod");
                }
                ad += inst->p_val;
                if (ad < 0 || ad >= T)
                        bug("invalid effective address");
                return ad;
        }

        /*
         *      simulator
         */

        simulate(pc_limit, global, pc)
                int pc_limit, global, pc;
        {
                /* initialize */
                if (global >= DIM(data))
                        fatal("Not enough room for global data.");
                T = global + 2;

                printf("\nExecution begins...\n\n");

                for (;;)
                {       /* fetch */
                        if (pc < 0 || pc >= pc_limit)
                                bug("pc not in program area");
                        inst = &prog[pc++];

                        /* decode operation and dispatch */
                        switch (inst->p_op) {
                        default:
                                printf("%d:\thalt\n", inst-prog);
                                return;
                        case OP_ALU:
                                if (T <= L+1)
                                        bug("simulator stack underflow");
                                switch (inst->p_mod) {
                                default:
                                        bug("illegal ALU instruction");
                                case ALU_ADD:   NEXT += TOP; break;
                                case ALU_SUB:   NEXT -= TOP; break;
                                case ALU_MUL:   NEXT *= TOP; break;
                                case ALU_DIV:   NEXT /= TOP; break;
                                case ALU_MOD:   NEXT %= TOP; break;
                                case ALU_LT:    NEXT = NEXT < TOP; break;
```

```
                case ALU_GT:    NEXT = NEXT > TOP; break;
                case ALU_LE:    NEXT = NEXT <= TOP; break;
                case ALU_GE:    NEXT = NEXT >= TOP; break;
                case ALU_EQ:    NEXT = NEXT == TOP; break;
                case ALU_NE:    NEXT = NEXT != TOP; break;
                case ALU_AND:   NEXT &= TOP; break;
                case ALU_OR:    NEXT |= TOP; break;
                case ALU_XOR:   NEXT ^= TOP; break;
                }
                POP;
                break;
        case OP_LOAD:
                if (T >= DIM(data))
                        fatal("Too much data.");
                if (inst->p_mod == MOD_IMMED)
                        PUSH = inst->p_val;
                else
                        PUSH = MEMORY;
                break;
        case OP_STORE:
                if (T <= L)
                        bug("simulator stack underflow");
                printf("%d:\tstore\t%d,%d\tto %d\n",
                        inst-prog, inst->p_mod,
                        inst->p_val, MEMORY = TOP);
                break;
        case OP_INC:
                if (T >= DIM(data))
                        fatal("Too much data.");
                printf("%d:\tinc\t%d,%d\tto %d\n",
                        inst-prog, inst->p_mod,
                        inst->p_val, PUSH = ++ MEMORY);
                break;

        case OP_DEC:
                if (T >= DIM(data))
                        fatal("Too much data.");
                printf("%d:\tdec\t%d,%d\tto %d\n",
                        inst-prog, inst->p_mod,
                        inst->p_val, PUSH = -- MEMORY);
                break;
        case OP_POP:
                if (T <= L)
                        bug("simulator stack underflow");
                POP;
                break;
        case OP_JUMP:
                printf("%d:\tjump\t%d\n", inst-prog,
                        inst->p_val);
                pc = inst->p_val;
                break;
        case OP_JUMPZ:
                if (T <= L)
                        bug("simulator stack underflow");
                if (data[POP] == 0)
                {       printf("%d:\tjumpz\t%d\n",
```

```
                                                inst-prog, inst->p_val);
                                    pc = inst->p_val;
                        }
                        break;
            case OP_CALL:
                        printf("%d:\tcall\t%d\n", inst-prog,
                                    inst->p_val);
                        PUSH = pc;
                        pc = inst->p_val;
                        PUSH = P;
                        P = T - 2 - inst->p_mod;
                        break;
            case OP_ENTRY:
                        PUSH = L;
                        L = T;
                        T += inst->p_val;
                        if (T >= DIM(data))
                                    fatal("Too much data.");
                        break;
            case OP_RETURN:
                        if (T < L)
                                    bug("simulator stack underflow");
                        T = L;
                        L = data[POP];
                        P = data[POP];
                        pc = data[POP];
                        printf("%d:\treturn\t%d to %d\n",
                                    inst-prog, RESULT, pc);
                        break;
            }
        }
    }
```

The code generation routines in *simgen.c* replace the corresponding routines in file *gen.c*, section A.6.

simgen.c

```
/*
 *      sample c -- code generator for simulator
 */

#include "sim.h"
#include "symtab.h"

/*
 *      program memory
 */
struct prog prog[L_PROG];
static int pc = 1;                    /* current program counter */
                                      /* HALT (0) is at address 0 */

/*
 *      generate a single instruction
 */

int gen(op, mod, val, comment)
```

```
        int op;                 /* operation code */
        int mod;                /* modifier */
        int val;                /* offset field */
        char * comment;         /* instruction comment */
{
        if (pc >= DIM(prog))
                fatal("Not enough program memory.");
        prog[pc].p_op = op;
        prog[pc].p_mod = mod;
        prog[pc].p_val = val;
        printf("%d:\t%d\t%d,%d\t; %s\n",
                pc, op, mod, val, comment);
        return pc ++;
}

/*
 *      region modifier
 */

int gen_mod(symbol)
        struct symtab * symbol;
{
        switch (symbol->s_blknum) {
        case 1:
                return MOD_GLOBAL;
        case 2:
                return MOD_PARAM;
        }
        return MOD_LOCAL;
}

/*
 *      general instructions
 */

gen_alu(mod, comment)
        int mod;                /* modifier */
        char * comment;         /* instruction comment */
{
        gen(OP_ALU, mod, 0, comment);
}

gen_li(const)
        char * const;           /* Constant value */
{
        gen(OP_LOAD, MOD_IMMED, atoi(const), const);
}

gen_pr(op, comment)
        int op;                 /* operation code */
        char * comment;         /* instruction comment */
{
        gen(op, 0, 0, comment);
}

/*
```

```
 *        generate jump, return target or chain
 */

int gen_jump(op, label, comment)
        int op;                  /* operation code */
        int label;               /* target of jump */
        char * comment;          /* instruction comment */
{       int pc = gen(op, 0, label, comment);

        if (label <= 0)
                return -pc;      /* new head of chain */
        else
                return label;    /* already defined */
}

/*
 *        generate tail of forward branch chain
 */

int new_label()
{
        return 0;                /* end of chain */
}

/*
 *        resolve forward branch chain
 */

int gen_label(chain)
        int chain;
{       int next;

        while (chain < 0)
        {       chain = - chain;
                next = prog[chain].p_val;
                if (next > 0)
                        break;   /* already ok */
                prog[chain].p_val = pc;
                printf("%d:\t(fixup)\t%d\n", chain, pc);
                chain = next;
        }
        return pc;
}

/*
 *        label stack manager
 */

static struct bc_stack {
        int bc_label;            /* label from new_label */
        struct bc_stack * bc_next;
        } * b_top,               /* head of break stack */
          * c_top;               /* head of continue stack */

static struct bc_stack * push(stack, label)
        struct bc_stack * stack;
```

```
                    int label;
    {               struct bc_stack * new_entry = (struct bc_stack *)
                            calloc(1, sizeof(struct bc_stack));

                    if (new_entry)
                    {       new_entry->bc_next = stack;
                            new_entry->bc_label = label;
                            return new_entry;
                    }
                    fatal("No more room to compile loops.");
                    /*NOTREACHED*/
    }

    static struct bc_stack * pop(stack)
                    struct bc_stack * stack;
    {               struct bc_stack * old_entry;

                    if (stack)
                    {       old_entry = stack;
                            stack = old_entry->bc_next;
                            cfree(old_entry);
                            return stack;
                    }
                    bug("break/continue stack underflow");
                    /*NOTREACHED*/
    }

    static int * top(stack)
                    struct bc_stack ** stack;
    {
                    if (! *stack)
                    {       error("no loop open");
                            *stack = push(*stack, 0);
                    }
                    return & (*stack) -> bc_label;
    }

    /*
     *      BREAK and CONTINUE
     */

    push_continue(label)
            int label;
    {
            c_top = push(c_top, label);
    }

    push_break(label)
            int label;
    {
            b_top = push(b_top, label);
    }

    gen_break()
    {
            *top(&b_top) = gen_jump(OP_JUMP, *top(&b_top), "BREAK");
```

```
        }

gen_continue()
{
        *top(&c_top) = gen_jump(OP_JUMP, *top(&c_top), "CONTINUE");
}

pop_break()
{
        gen_label(*top(&b_top));
        b_top = pop(b_top);
}

pop_continue()
{
        gen_label(*top(&c_top));
        c_top = pop(c_top);
}

/*
 *      function call
 */

gen_call(symbol, count)
        struct symtab * symbol; /* function */
        int     count;          /* # of arguments */
{       int pc;

        chk_parm(symbol, count);
        pc = gen(OP_CALL, count, symbol->s_offset, symbol->s_name);
        if (symbol->s_offset <= 0)
                symbol->s_offset = -pc; /* head of chain */
        while (count-- > 0)
                gen_pr(OP_POP, "pop argument");
        gen(OP_LOAD, MOD_GLOBAL, 0, "push result");
}

/*
 *      function prologue and definition
 */

int gen_entry(symbol)
        struct symtab * symbol; /* function */
{
        symbol->s_offset = gen_label(symbol->s_offset);
        gen(OP_ENTRY, 0, 0, symbol->s_name);
        return symbol->s_offset;
}

fix_entry(symbol, label)
        struct symtab * symbol; /* function */
        int label;
{       extern int l_max;       /* size of local region */

        prog[label].p_val = l_max;
        printf("%d:\tentry\t%d\t; %s\n",
```

```
                    label, l_max, symbol->s_name);
}


/*
 *      wrap-up
 */

end_program()
{       extern int g_offset;      /* size of global region */
        extern struct symtab * s_find();
        int main = s_find("main") -> s_offset;

        all_program();            /* allocate global variables */
        printf("%d:\tend\t%d,%d\n", pc, g_offset, main);
        simulate(pc, g_offset, main);
}
```

A load-and-go compiler and simulator for our fictitious machine can be compiled using the following command:

```
cc sim.c simgen.c mem.c symtab.c message.c y.tab.c lex.yy.c \
        colib -ll -o sim
```

A.8 Improved error messages from "yaccpar"

The error messages issued by a *yacc* parser can be improved. *yacc* builds a parser using a model stored in the file */usr/lib/yaccpar*. The normal behavior of *yaccpar* in case of an error is:

```
switch (yyerrflag) {
case 0:                                 /* brand new error */
        yyerror("syntax error");
yyerrlab:
        ++yynerrs;
case 1:                                 /* incompletely recovered */
case 2:                                 /* ... try again */
        yyerrflag = 3;
        ...
```

The switch is reached if the transition matrix contains the error operation. At this point the message syntax error is issued, regardless of the actual nature of the error.

yyerrflag is used to avoid cascades of messages. It is normally zero. If there is an error, it is set to three. During each shift operation, yyerrflag is counted down. An error message is only issued if yyerrflag is zero.

We can attempt to improve the error message as follows: in the current state, we should consider *all possible* terminal symbols in place of the actual input, to discover those for which the transition matrix does not contain the error action. A suitably formatted list of these symbols can be issued in place of the simple syntax error message.

/usr/lib/yaccpar is always available in source. We compute the desired list of symbols essentially by copying the algorithm employed by the model parser for actual input:

```
        switch (yyerrflag) {
        case 0:                              /* brand new error */
                if ((yyn = yypact[yystate]) > YYFLAG && yyn < YYLAST)
                {       register int x;

                        for (x = yyn>0? yyn: 0; x < YYLAST; ++x)
                                if (yychk[yyact[x]] == x - yyn
                                    && x - yyn != YYERRCODE)
                                        yyerror(0, yydisplay(x-yyn));
                }
                yyerror(0,0);
        yyerrlab:
                ++yynerrs;
                . . .
```

yystate is the current state, YYLAST is the extent of the transition matrix encoded as yyact[], and yyin is a temporary variable used by *yaccpar*. yypact[] is a filter to exclude certain simple cases. This information is provided by *yacc*.

If we are in a situation where yyact[] is actually inspected, we let x range over all possible indices into yyact[]. These must at least be zero, and the algorithm in *yaccpar* shows that they must also exceed yypact[yystate]. If we find a value for x which does not correspond to the error symbol YYERRCODE and which would not produce an error operation from yyact[], we display the corresponding input symbol.

If a list of possible input symbols can be computed in this fashion, *yaccpar* issues a call

```
        yyerror(0,t)
```

for each terminal symbol t in the list; t is represented as a character string. The end of the list is indicated by a call

```
        yyerror(0,0)
```

This call is also issued if the list cannot be computed. yyerror() can be extended as follows to produce improved error messages:

```
        /*
         *      yyerror() -- [detailed] error message for yyparse()
         */

        #include <stdio.h>

        FILE * yyerfp = stdout;        /* error stream */

                                       /*VARARGS1*/
        yyerror(s,t)                   /* "message" or 0,"token" */
                register char * s, * t;
        {       extern int yynerrs;    /* total number of errors */
                static int list = 0;   /* sequential calls */

                if (s || ! list)       /* header necessary?? */
                {       fprintf(yyerfp, "[error %d] ", yynerrs+1);
                        yywhere();
                        if (s)         /* simple message?? */
                        {       fputs(s, yyerfp);
```

```
                                putc('\n', yyerfp);
                                return;
                        }
                        if (t)              /* first token?? */
                        {       fputs("expecting: ", yyerfp);
                                fputs(t, yyerfp);
                                list = 1;
                                return;
                        }
                                        /* no tokens acceptable */
                        fputs("syntax error\n", yyerfp);
                        return;
                }
                if (t)                  /* subsequent token?? */
                {       putc(' ', yyerfp);
                        fputs(t, yyerfp);
                        return;
                }
                                        /* end of enhanced message */
                putc('\n', yyerfp);
                list = 0;
        }
```

The implementation of the new error message expecting: *symbols* in yyerror() is quite simple. Basically we dispatch different calls depending on the presence of null pointers. The static variable list maintains its value between successive calls; it is used to distinguish the first terminal symbol in a series from the remaining symbols so that an appropriate message header may be issued.

In *yaccpar* we have employed a function yydisplay() which must convert the encoding of a symbol as an integer into a printable string:

```
#include <ctype.h>
#define DIM(x)  (sizeof x / sizeof x[0])

static char * yydisplay(ch)
        register int ch;
{       static char buf[15];
        static char * token[] = {
#include "y.tok.h"                     /* token names */
                0 };

        switch(ch) {
        case 0:
                return "[end of file]";
        case YYERRCODE:
                return "[error]";
        case '\b':
                return "'\\b'";
        case '\f':
                return "'\\f'";
        case '\n':
                return "'\\n'";
        case '\r':
                return "'\\r'";
        case '\t':
```

```
                return "'\\t'";
        }
        if (ch > 256 && ch < 256 + DIM(token))
                return token[ch - 257];
        if (isascii(ch) && isprint(ch))
                sprintf(buf, "'%c'", ch);
        else if (ch < 256)
                sprintf(buf, "char %04.3o", ch);
        else
                sprintf(buf, "token %d", ch);
        return buf;
}
```

If the symbol ch is a printable ASCII character or if it can be represented by a control character escape sequence, we show the corresponding C-style character constant. If the symbol value exceeds 256, it was normally defined by *yacc* in reponse to a %token statement; in this case we try to decode it using an array token[] with appropriate character strings. If neither approach is possible, we return the numerical value. The entire function yydisplay() should be inserted near the beginning of the file */usr/lib/yaccpar*; it can also be used to improve the output generated under the YYDEBUG option.

The following shell procedure can be used to construct the entries for the token[] vector from the file *y.tab.h*:

```
grep '^#.*define' y.tab.h \
| sed 's/^# define \([^ ]*\) [^ ]*$/    "\1",/'   > y.tok.h
```

The strings are placed into a file *y.tok.h*. So that things work even if the file does not exist, an empty file */usr/include/y.tok.h* should be present in the system to be included for yydisplay() as a default.

The new version of yyerror() shown here and the functions which were shown in section 3.3 are best collected into a library *colib* as follows:

```
cc -c main.c cpp.c yywhere.c yyerror.c
ar r colib main.o cpp.o yywhere.o yyerror.o
ranlib colib
```

A.9 Improved debugging output from "yaccpar"

Debugging output from */usr/lib/yaccpar* also can be improved. One fairly essential defect is the fact that some inputs are used and discarded *before* they are displayed. The basic architecture of *yaccpar* in this respect is as follows:

```
#ifdef  YYDEBUG
int yydebug = 0;
#endif
int yychar;      /* current input token number */

yyparse()
{       register short yystate;
        ...
        yychar = -1;
```

```
yystack:              /* put a state and value onto the stack */

#ifdef  YYDEBUG
        if (yydebug)
                printf("state %d, char 0%o\n", yystate, yychar);
#endif


        ...
        if (yychar < 0)            /* lookahead available? */
                if ((yychar = yylex()) < 0)
                        yychar = 0;     /* end of file */
        ...
        if ( /* valid shift */ )
        {       ...
                yychar = -1;
                goto yystack;
        }
        ...
```

In order to improve things, we need to print each terminal symbol as soon as it is obtained from yylex(). Since the nested if statements above appear twice in *yaccpar*, it is best to replace them by calling a new routine yyylex() defined as follows:

```
static yyylex()
{
        if (yychar < 0)
        {       if ((yychar = yylex ()) < 0)
                        yychar = 0;
#ifdef YYDEBUG
        if (yydebug)
                printf("[yydebug] reading %s\n",
                        yydisplay(yychar));
#endif
        }
}
```

where we have used yydisplay() to construct a reasonably legible representation of the terminal symbol.

A.10 Regression testing

One should generally save the input files used to test the compiler during development. If the compiler is changed, the test files can be run again to ascertain that at least some of the old features of the compiler are still functioning. The following Bourne shell script automates this testing procedure:

```
        if test ! -d $OD
        then    mkdir $OD
        fi

        for i in $ID/*
        do      file='basename $i'
                "$@" $i >$OD/\&$file
                echo end of task code $? >>$OD/\&$file
                if test -r $OD/$file
                then    if cmp -s $OD/\&$file $OD/$file
                        then    echo "$1 $file unchanged"
                                rm $OD/\&$file
                        else    echo "$1 $file changed: <new >old"
                                diff $OD/\&$file $OD/$file
                                mv $OD/$file $OD/${file}_old
                                mv $OD/\&$file $OD/$file
                        fi
                else    echo "$1 $file created"
                        mv $OD/\&$file $OD/$file
                fi
        done
        exit 0
```

$ID must be defined as the name of the directory containing the test files. Similarly, $OD is the name of the directory containing the output files produced for each of the test files. Each test file and corresponding output file have the same name in each directory. Temporary file names start with &. If the current and previous versions of an output file differ, the previous version is saved using the suffix _old.

The shell procedure is called with the name of the processor to be tested, optionally followed by arguments to be passed to the processor prior to a test file name. The procedure takes each test file in turn, runs the processor, and compares the output with the previous output. If the outputs are equal, the previous output is retained (to preserve the time stamp in the file hierarchy). If the outputs differ, the difference is shown using *diff*. If no previous output exists, this fact is reported, too.

The procedure assumes that the processor to be tested accepts a file name argument for the input file. This is not the case for a program generated with *lex* which uses the main() function from the *lex* library. For this case the processor call may be revised to

```
        "$@" <$i >$OD/\&$file
```

"$@" is employed as the call to the processor so that all arguments passed to the shell procedure are passed on to the processor unchanged, even if they contain white space.

References

[Aho74]   A. V. Aho and S. C. Johnson, "LR Parsing," *Comp. Surveys*, vol. 6, no. 2, pp. 99-124, June 1974.

[Aho77]   A. V. Aho and J. D. Ullman, *Principles of Compiler Design*, Addison-Wesley, Reading, Mass., 1977.

[Bau76]   F. L. Bauer and J. Eickel (ed.), *Compiler Construction: An Advanced Course*, Springer, Berlin, 1974, 1976.

[Gra79]   S. L. Graham, C. B. Haley, and W. N. Joy, "Practical LR error recovery," *SIGPLAN Notices*, Aug 1979.

[Gri71]   D. Gries, *Compiler Construction for Digital Computers*, Wiley, New York, 1971.

[Jen75]   K. Jensen and N Wirth, *Pascal: User Manual and Report*, Springer, Berlin, 1975.

[Joh78]   S. C. Johnson, "Yacc: Yet Another Compiler-Compiler," in [Ker78a].

[Ker78a]   B. W. Kernighan and M. D. McIlroy, *UNIX Programmer's Manual*, Bell Laboratories, 1978. Seventh Edition.

[Ker78b]   B. W. Kernighan and D. M. Ritchie, *The C Programming Language*, Prentice-Hall, Englewood Cliffs, New Jersey, 1978.

[Les78a]   M. E. Lesk, "Typing Documents on the UNIX System: Using the -ms Macros with Troff and Nroff," in [Ker78a].

[Les78b]   M. E. Lesk and E. Schmidt, "Lex: A Lexical Analyzer Generator," in [Ker78a].

[Nau63]   P. Naur (ed.), "Revised Report on the Algorithmic Language Algol 60," *CACM*, pp. 1-17, Jan. 1963.

[Wic73]   B. A. Wichman, "The Definition of Comments in Programming Languages," NPL Report NAC-34, National Physics Laboratory, Division of Numerical Analysis and Computing, Teddington, England, May 1973.

[Wij75]   A. van Wijngaarden, B. J. Mailloux, J. E. L. Peck, C. H. A. Koster, M. Sintzoff, C. H. Lindsey, L. G. L. T. Meertens, and R. G. Fisker, "Revised Report on the Algorithmic Language Algol 68," *Acta Informatica*, pp. 1-236, 1, 1975.

[Wir77]   N. Wirth, *Compilerbau*, B. G. Teubner, Stuttgart, 1977.

[Wir82]   N. Wirth, *Programming in Modula-2*, Springer, Berlin, 1982.

Index